und Andere, G. Careless

The Latter-day Saints' Psalmody

und Andere, G. Careless
The Latter-day Saints' Psalmody
ISBN/EAN: 9783744783828

Printed in Europe, USA, Canada, Australia, Japan

Cover: Foto ©Thomas Meinert / pixelio.de

More available books at **www.hansebooks.com**

und Andere, G. Careless

The Latter-day Saints' Psalmody

ISBN/EAN: 9783744783828

Printed in Europe, USA, Canada, Australia, Japan

Cover: Foto ©Thomas Meinert / pixelio.de

More available books at **www.hansebooks.com**

⁓THE⁓

LATTER-DAY SAINTS'
PSALMODY.

A COLLECTION OF ORIGINAL TUNES

Composed and Compiled by the following Committee:

G. CARELESS, E. BEESLEY, J. J. DAYNES, E. STEPHENS, T. C. GRIGGS,

ALSO EMBRACING COMPOSITIONS OF OTHER WELL KNOWN COMPOSERS,

TOGETHER WITH

A ❧ Number ❧ of ❧ Old ❧ and ❧ Familiar ❧ Tunes

SPECIALLY ARRANGED FOR THIS WORK,

PROVIDING MUSIC FOR EVERY HYMN IN THE L. D. S. HYMN BOOK.

GOTTEN UP UNDER THE APPROVAL OF THE LATE PRESIDENT JOHN TAYLOR, AND ACCEPTED BY PRESIDENT WILFORD WOODRUFF AND COUNCIL, FOR THE USE OF THE MEMBERS OF THE CHURCH OF JESUS CHRIST OF LATTER-DAY SAINTS.

SALT LAKE CITY, UTAH:
PUBLISHED BY THE DESERET NEWS COMPANY.
1889.

COMPILERS' PREFACE.

THE origination (by the approval of the late President John Taylor) and completion (to the acceptance of the First Presidency of the Church) of this the largest and most important musical work yet published in Utah, has been to the undersigned a labor of love and principle. Our aim has been to present a suitable and acceptable tune for every hymn in the Latter-day Saints' Hymn Book. We have been materially aided by the contributions of those who have so readily placed their appreciated compositions at our disposal.

The original music, with some few exceptions, is the production of "our mountain home" composers.

Another feature which we feel confident will prove acceptable to many, is the presentation of a number of old and familiar tunes, which, together with the words, are associated by many with incidents of the most pleasing experience in their first acquaintance with the Gospel; while to others, scenes of trial and suffering will be vividly brought to their remembrance.

That this work may be a means of still further extending a knowledge of the Gospel of salvation; an aid to the congregations of the Saints in singing the praises of the Lord and of assistance in their gatherings the world over, is the prayer of your brethren in the Gospel of peace.

GEORGE CARELESS,
EBENEZER BEESLEY,
JOSEPH J. DAYNES,
EVAN STEPHENS,
THOMAS C. GRIGGS.

SALT LAKE CITY, UTAH, U. S. A.,
May 27th, 1889.

PUBLISHERS' PREFACE.

THE PSALMODY here presented is by far the largest and most costly musical work ever published in Utah or for the Church of Jesus Christ of Latter-day Saints. It has been thought, however, that the demand for it would be sufficient to warrant the expenditure required, which has been a large amount. If the sale of the Hymn Book for which the Psalmody supplies the music may be accepted as a criterion, the expectation concerning this work will probably not prove unfounded, for many large editions of that book have been published and sold.

That our efforts to cater to the growing musical taste of the community may be appreciated and the Psalmody find a ready sale and fulfill all the expectations concerning it, is the earnest hope of its publishers.

THE DESERET NEWS CO.

THE
LATTER-DAY SAINTS'
PSALMODY.

No. 1   ANIMATION. L. M. [Page 266.]   E. BEESLEY.

1. The hap-py day has roll-ed on, The truth re-stored is now made known, The prom-ised an-gel's come a-gain To in-tro-duce Mes-si-ah's reign.
2. The gos-pel trump a-gain is heard, The truth from dark-ness has ap-peared The lands which long be-night-ed lay, Have now be-held a glorious day.
3. The day by pro-phets long fore-told, The day which A-bra'm did be-hold, The day the Saints de-sired so long, When God His strange work would per-form.
4. The day when Saints a-gain shall hear The voice of Je-sus in their ear, And an-gels, who a-bove do reign, Come down to con-verse hold with men.

1. When earth in bondage long had lain, And darkness o'er the nations reign'd
2. A voice commissioned from on high, Hark! Hark! it is the angel's cry,
3. He comes the gos-pel to re-veal In fullness to be-nighted man;
4. Translat-ed by the power of God, His voice bears record to His word;
5. Restored the Priesthood, long since lost, In truth and power as at the first:
6. Bap-tiz-ing those who did be-lieve, That they the Spi-rit might recieve

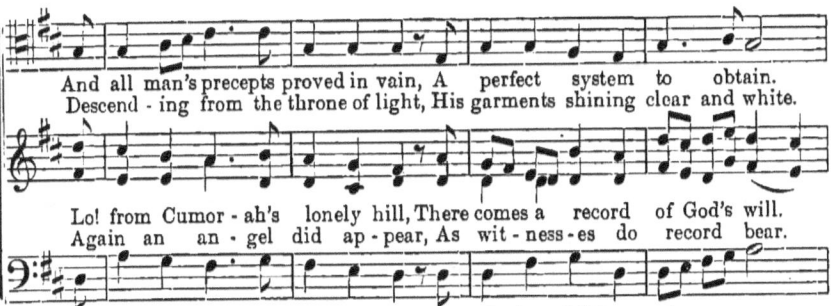

And all man's precepts proved in vain, A perfect system to obtain.
Descend-ing from the throne of light, His garments shining clear and white.
Lo! from Cumor-ah's lonely hill, There comes a record of God's will.
Again an an-gel did ap-pear, As wit-ness-es do record bear.
Thus men commissioned from on high, Came forth and did repentance cry.
In ful-ness as in days of old, And have one Shepherd and one fold.

A perfect sys-tem to obtain, A perfect sys-tem to ob-tain.
His garments shin-ing clear and white, His garments shining clear and white.
There comes a re-cord of God's will, There comes a re-cord of God's will.
As witnesses do record bear, As witnesses do re-cord bear.
Came forth and did, repentance cry Came forth and did re-pent-ance cry.
And have one Shep-herd and one fold, And have one Shepherd and one fold.

COMMUNION. (Concluded.)

No. 21.   CHINA. L. M. [Page 230.]   B. CUZENS.

1. Great God! to thee my evening song With humble grati-tude I raise; O let thy mer-cy tune my tongue, O let thy mer-cy tune my tongue, And fill my heart with lively praise
2. My days, uncloud-ed as they pass, And ev-ery on-ward roll-ing hour, Are mon-u-ments of won-d'rous grace, Are mon-u-ments of won-d'rous grace, And witness to thy love and power.
3. And yet this thoughtless, wretched heart, Too oft re-gard-less of thy love, Ungrateful can from thee de-part, Un-grateful can from thee de-part And from the path of duty rove.

No. 23.   EMERY. L. M. [Page 404.]   HENRY EMERY.

HEBER. (Concluded.)

No. 33.　　　　　　　HUDSON. L. M. [Page 5.]　　　　G. CARELESS.
Moderato.

1. The morning breaks, the shad-ows flee; Lo! Zi-on's stand-ard
2. The clouds of er-ror dis-ap-pear Be-fore the rays of
3. The Gen-tile ful-ness now comes in, And Is-rael's bless-ings

is un-furled! The dawn-ing of a brighter day The dawn-ing
truth di-vine; The glo-ry, bursting from a-far, The glo-ry
are at hand: Lo! Ju-dah's remnant, cleansed from sin, Lo! Ju-dah's

of a bright-er day Ma-jes-tic ris-es on the world.
burst-ing from a-far, Wide o'er the na-tions soon will shine.
remnant, cleansed from sin, Shall in their prom-ised Canaan stand.

No. 43.   JONATHAN. L. M. [Page 97.]   HANDEL.

KINDNESS. (Concluded.)

No. 47. KIMBALL. L. M. [Page 146.] JOS. J. DAYNES.

MEMORY. (Concluded.)

sleep, which still will fly, Then shall re - flec - tion's
stream of mem - 'ry glide; And all the past, a

wrap the sul - len sky, I muse on life's tem -
bright-er pow'r Il - lume the lone and mid - night hour.
gen - tle train Wak'd by re - mem - brance, live a - gain.
pest - uous sea, And sigh, O Lord, to come to thee.

No. 53. MOTHER. L. M. [Page 186.] GEO. CARELESS.

1. The morning flow'rs display their sweets, And gay their silken leaves un-fold,
2. Nipt by the wind's un-kind-ly blast, Parc'd by the sun's di - rect - er ray,
3. So blooms the hu-man face di-vine, When youth its pride of beau - ty shows,

As careless of the noon-tide heats, As fear - less of the ev'n - ing cold.
The mo-ment-ar-y glo-ries waste, The short-lived beau-ties die a - way.
Fairer than spring the col-ors shine, And sweet- er than the vir - gin rose.

No. 55.   MALACHI. L. M. [Page 26.]   GEO. CARELESS.

No. 58. PERU. L. M. [Page 39.] J. LEACH.

1* Also page 140.

PERU. (Concluded.)

No. 59.   PETER. L. M. [Page 230.]   JAS. P. OLSEN.

1. Haste glo-rious day, when Christ shall come To reign su-preme o'er land and sea, When saints shall all be gath-ered home, And earth be ruled with e-qui-ty.

# No. 61. PREPARATION. L. M. [Page 197.] JOS. J. DAYNES.

No. 64. RESTORATION. L. M. [Page 188.] G. CARELESS.

REDEMPTION. (Concluded.)

powers ar - ray A - gainst the Prince of life and light, And Jud - as
sol - emn word, "There's one of you as- sem - bled here Who will this
brake and blest; "If I," said he, "be lift - ed up, The pen - i -
did his Lord be - tray! And Jud - as did his Lord be - tray!
night be - tray his Lord!" Who will this night be - tray his Lord!"
tent shall share my rest." The pen - i - tent shall share my rest."

No. 68.   **RELIEF. L. M.** [Page 220.]   G. CARELESS.

1. Un-veil thy bo - som, faith-ful tomb; Take this new trea-sure to thy trust!
2. Nor pain, nor grief, nor an-xious fear, In - vade thy bounds; no mor- tal woes
3. So Jes - us slept; God's dy - ing Son Passed thro' the grave and blest the bed!

And give these sa - cred rel - ics room To slum - ber in the si - lent dust.
Can reach the peace - ful sleep-er here, While an - gels watch the soft re - pose.
Rest here, blest Saint, till from his throne The morning breaks to pierce the shade.

1. Though deep'ning tri - als throng your way, Press on, press on, ye Saints of God! Ere long the res - ur - rec - tion day Will spread its light and truth a - broad. Will spread its light and truth a - broad.
2. Though out-ward ills a - wait us here, The time at long - est is not long Ere Jes - us Christ will re - ap - pear, Sur - round-ed by a glo - rious throng. Sur- round-ed by a glo - rious throng.
3. Lift up your hearts in praise to God— Let your re - joic - ings nev - er cease: Tho' trib - u - la - tions rage a - broad, Christ says, "In me ye shall have peace." Christ says "In me ye shall have peace."

No. 70.   ST. GEORGE. L. M. [Page 9.]   JOS. J. DAYNES.

1. The time is nigh, that hap - py time, That great, ex-pect-ed, bless - ed day,
2. The proph-e- sies must be ful- filled, Tho' earth and hell should dare op-pose
3. Soon shall the blend-ed im - age fall— Brass, sil-ver, i - ron, gold and clay;

SANCTITY. (Concluded.)

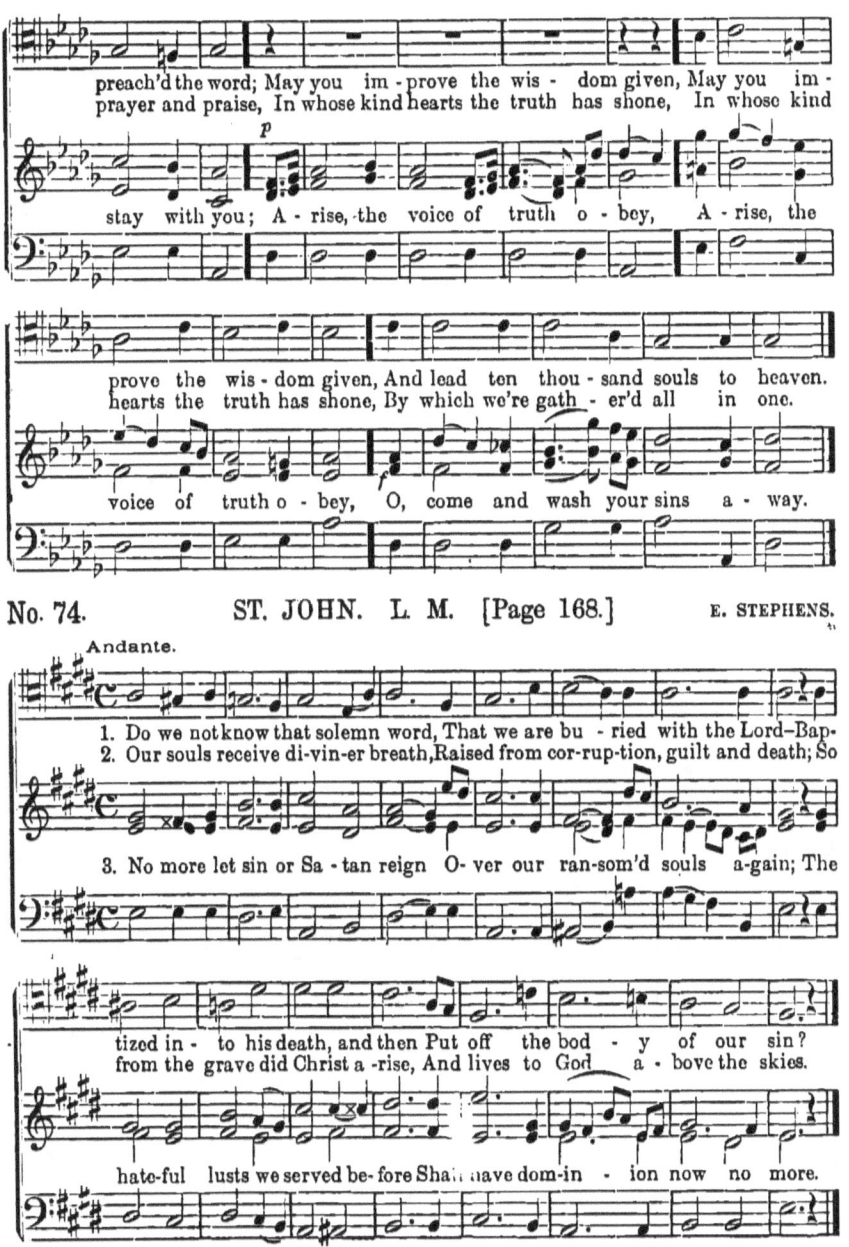

No. 74.   ST. JOHN. L. M. [Page 168.]   E. STEPHENS.

Andante.

1. Do we not know that solemn word, That we are bu-ried with the Lord—Baptized in-to his death, and then Put off the bod-y of our sin?
2. Our souls receive di-vin-er breath, Raised from cor-rup-tion, guilt and death; So from the grave did Christ a-rise, And lives to God a-bove the skies.
3. No more let sin or Sa-tan reign O-ver our ran-som'd souls a-gain; The hate-ful lusts we served be-fore Shall have dom-in-ion now no more.

# No. 76. SAMSON. L. M. [Page 77.] HANDEL.

No. 82. VERNON. L. M. [Page 104.] JOS. J. DAYNES.

No. 85. WINDSOR. L. M. [Page 272.] W. C. CLIVE.

WINDSOR. (Concluded.)

No. 86. W. X. L. M. [Page 315.] T. C. GRIGGS.

EUCHARIST. (Concluded.)

No. 90. COMFORT. 6-8's. [Page 395.] HAYDN.

1. Cease, ye fond par-ents, cease to weep; Let grief no more your bo-som swell; For what is death? 'Tis na-ture's sleep: The trump of God will break its spell! For He, whose arm is strong to save, A-rose in tri-umph o'er the grave.

2. Why should you sor-row? Death is sweet To those who die in Jes-us' love; Though called to part, you soon shall meet In ho-lier, hap-pier climes a-bove; For all the faith-ful Christ will save, And crown with vict-'ry o'er the grave.

3. There's con-so-la-tion in the blow, Al-though it crush a ten-der tie; For while it lays its vic-tims low, Death o-pens to the worlds on high; Ce-les-tial glo-ries proud-ly wave A-bove the con-fines of the grave.

No. 96.   PROVIDENCE. 6-8s. [Page 27.]   G. CARELESS.
Andante.

CHORISTER. (Concluded.)

fly The hosts of dark-ness fly, Up-held by whose e-ter-nal
wave, Must curb each flash-ing wave, Own-ing thy voice when sur-ges

sea, Who, o'er yon dark blue sea, Self-ex-iled from their na-tive

hand, Thy saints can dare or die,— Thy saints can dare or die,—
sweep De-struc-tion round the brave.— De-struc-tion round the brave.—

land, Are borne to wor-ship thee! Are borne to wor-ship thee!

No. 109.　　CHARITY. C. M. [Page 402.]　　G. CARELESS.

Andante.

1. O Lord of Hosts, we now in-voke Thy spir-it most di-vine,
2. May we for-ev-er think of thee, And of thy suff-'rings sore,
3. Pre-pare our minds, that we may see The beaut-ies of thy grace;

To cleanse our hearts while we par-take The bro-ken bread and wine.
En-dured for us on Cal-va-ry, And praise thee ev-er-more.
Sal-va-tion pur-chased on that tree For all who seek thy face.

No. 119.   FORGIVENESS. C. M. [Page 81.]   JOS. J. DAYNES.

1. How are thy serv-ants blest! O Lord, How sure is their de-fence! Eternal wis-dom is their guide, Eternal wis-dom is their guide, Their help, Om-nip-o-tence.
2. In for-eign realms and lands re-mote, Sup-port-ed by thy care, Through burn-ing climes they pass un-hurt, Through burn-ing climes they pass un-hurt, And breathe in taint-ed air.
3. When by the dread-ful temp-est borne High on the bro-ken wave, They know thou art not slow to hear, They know thou art not slow to hear, Nor im-po-tent to save.

No. 120.   FORTITUDE. C. M. [Page 182.]   J. P. OLSEN.

1. Let those who would be Saints in-deed Fear not what oth-ers
2. What tho' the storm-clouds gath-er dark,—Look up and trust in
3. Fear not the dark-ness of the night, But move with care-ful

GOOD TIDINGS. (Concluded.)

No. 124. GRATITUDE. C. M. [Page 227.] T. C. GRIGGS

1. Come, let us sing an ev'n-ing hymn, To calm our minds for rest; And each one try, with sin-gle eye, To praise the Sav-ior best. To praise the Sav-ior best.
2. Yes, let us sing a sa-cred song, To close the pass-ing day; With one ac-cord call on the Lord, And ev-er watch and pray. And ev-er watch and pray.
3. O, thank the Lord for grace and gifts Re-newed in lat-ter days— For truth and light to guide us right In wis-dom's pleas-ant ways; In wis-dom's pleas-ant ways;

No. 126.   HANNAH. C. M. [Page 398.]   E. STEPHENS.

1. Lift up your hends, ye scat-ter'd Saints, Re-demp-tion
2. The blood of those who have been slain For ven-geance
3. The signs in heav'n and earth ap-pear, And blood and

draw-eth nigh; Our Sav-ior hears the or-phan's
cries a-loud; Nor shall its cries as-cend in
smoke and fire; Men's hearts are fail-ing them for

plaints, Our Sav-ior hears the or-phan's plaints The widow's mournful cry.
vain Nor shall its cries as-cend in vain For vengeance on the proud.
fear, Men's hearts are fail-ing them for fear, Re-demp-tion's draw-ing nigher.

No. 131. INCARNATION. C. M. [Page 21.] DR. RIPPON.

1. Mor-tals, a-wake! with an-gels join, And chant the
2. In heav'n the rap-turous song be-gan, And sweet se-
3. The theme, the song, the joy was new, To each an-

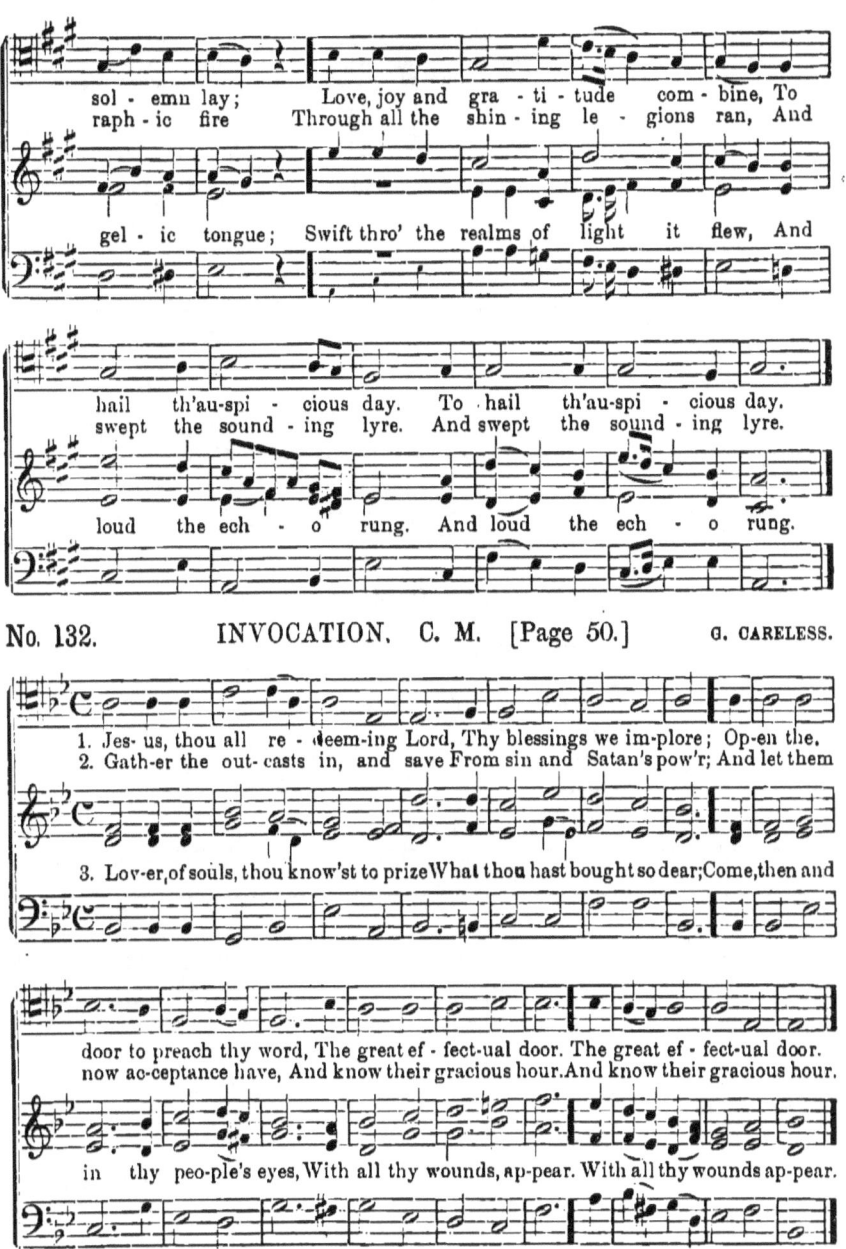

MOUNT ZION. (Continued.)

MOUNT ZION. (Concluded.)

ZION'S HILL. (Concluded.)

No. 163. ADOPTION. C. M. D. [Page 91.] JOHN S. LEWIS.

ADOPTION. (Concluded.)

No. 166.   FAREWELL.   C. M. D.   [Page 239.]

No. 171. SELAH. C. M. D. [Page 413.] JOS. J. DAYNES.

Not too fast.

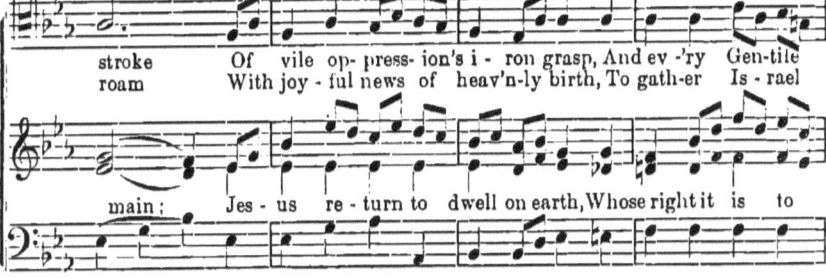

1. O Lord, pre-serve thy chos-en seed! They've keen-ly felt the
2. Thy ser-vants, too, pre-serve from harm, As through the earth they
3. May light di-vine shed forth its ray, And with the pure re-

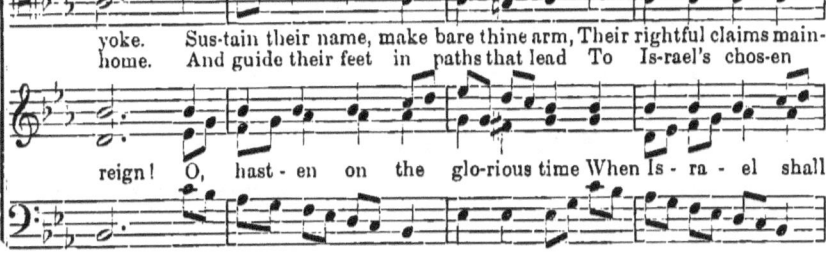

stroke Of vile op-press-ion's i-ron grasp, And ev-'ry Gen-tile
roam With joy-ful news of heav'n-ly birth, To gath-er Is-rael
main; Jes-us re-turn to dwell on earth, Whose right it is to

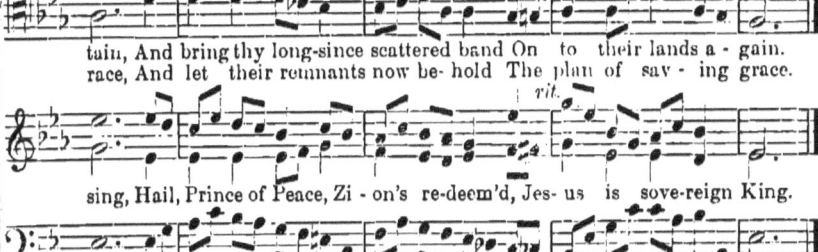

yoke. Sus-tain their name, make bare thine arm, Their rightful claims main-
home. And guide their feet in paths that lead To Is-rael's chos-en
reign! O, hast-en on the glo-rious time When Is-ra-el shall

tain, And bring thy long-since scattered band On to their lands a-gain.
race, And let their remnants now be-hold The plan of sav-ing grace.
sing, Hail, Prince of Peace, Zi-on's re-deem'd, Jes-us is sove-reign King.

rit.

No. 173. ATONEMENT. S. M. [Page 53.] GEO. CARELESS.

Andante.

1. Spir-it of faith, come down, Re-veal the things of God, And
2. 'Tis thine the blood t'ap-ply, And give us eyes to see; Who
3. No man can tru-ly say That Jes-us is the Lord, Un-

make to us the God-head known, And wit-ness with the blood.
did for ev-'ry sin-ner die, Did sure-ly die for me.
less thou take the veil a-way, And breathe the liv-ing word.

No. 174. AGNES. S. M. [Page 18.] E. STEPHENS.

Moderato.

1. Let sin-ners take their course, And choose the road to death; But
2. My thoughts ad-dress his throne When morn-ing brings the light; I
3. Thou wilt re-gard my cries, O my E-ter-nal God! While

in the wor-ship of my God I'll spend my dai-ly breath.
seek his bless-ings ev-'ry noon, And pay my vows at night.
sin-ners per-ish in sur-prise, Be-neath thine ang-ry rod.

No. 176.   BISHOP. S. M.   [Page 86.]   JOHN TULLIDGE.

No. 182.   SATURN. S. M. [Page 11.]   JOS. J. DAYNES.

No. 187. CUMORAH. JOHN TULLIDGE.
4-6s & 2-8s. [Page 218.]

Andante con moto.
TRIO.

1. An an-gel from on high, The long, long silence broke; De-scend-ing from the sky, These gra-cious words he spoke—
2. Seal'd by Mo-ro-ni's hand, It has for a-ges lain, To wait the Lord's com-mand, From dust to speak a-gain.
3. It speaks of Jos-eph's seed, And makes the rem-nant known Of na-tion's long since dead, Who once had dwelt a-lone.

CHORUS. Allegro animato.

Lo! in Cu-mo-rah's lone-ly hill, A sa-cred re-cord lies con-ceal'd.
It shall a-gain to light come forth, To ush-er in Christ's reign on earth.
The ful-ness of the Gos-pel, too, Its pa-ges will re-veal to view.

Lo! in Cu-mo-rah's lone-ly hill, A sa-cred re-cord lies con-ceal'd.
It shall a-gain to light come forth, To ush-er in Christ's reign on earth.
The ful-ness of the Gos-pel, too, Its pa-ges will re-veal to view.

No. 189.   COVENANT.   JOS. J. DAYNES.
4-6s & 2-8s. [Page 181.]
Maestoso.

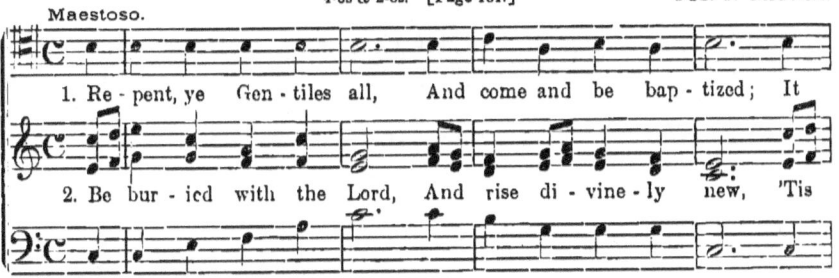

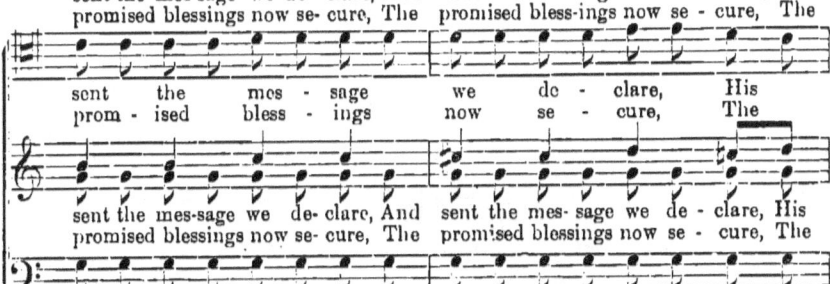
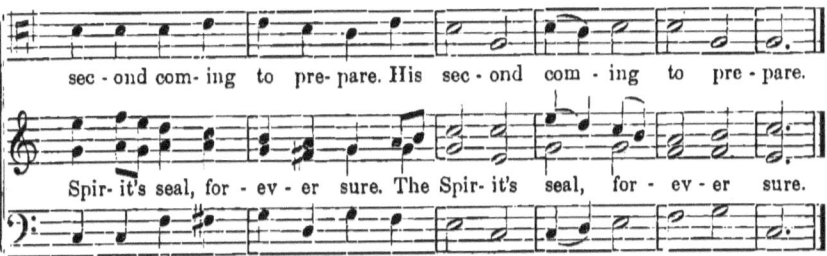

No. 190. COMPASSION.

4-6s & 2-8s. [Page 152.]

G. CARELESS.

No. 191. DIVINITY.

4-6s & 2-8s. [Page 174.]

S. B. POND.

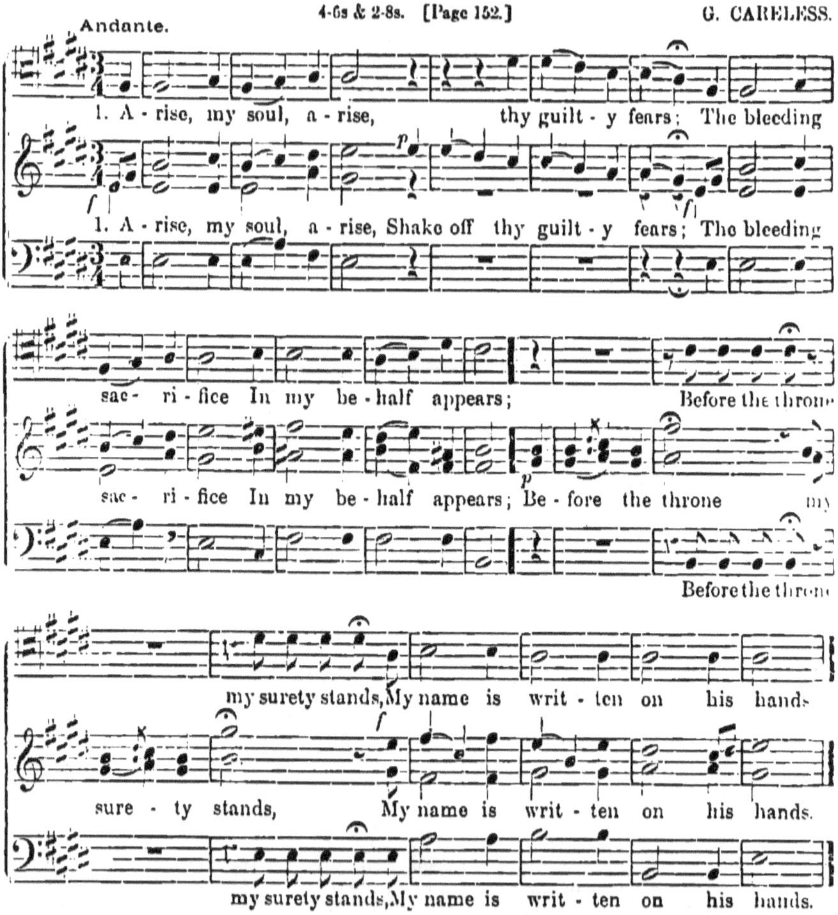

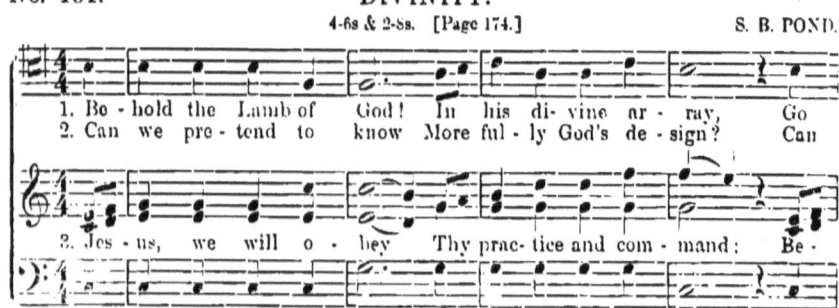

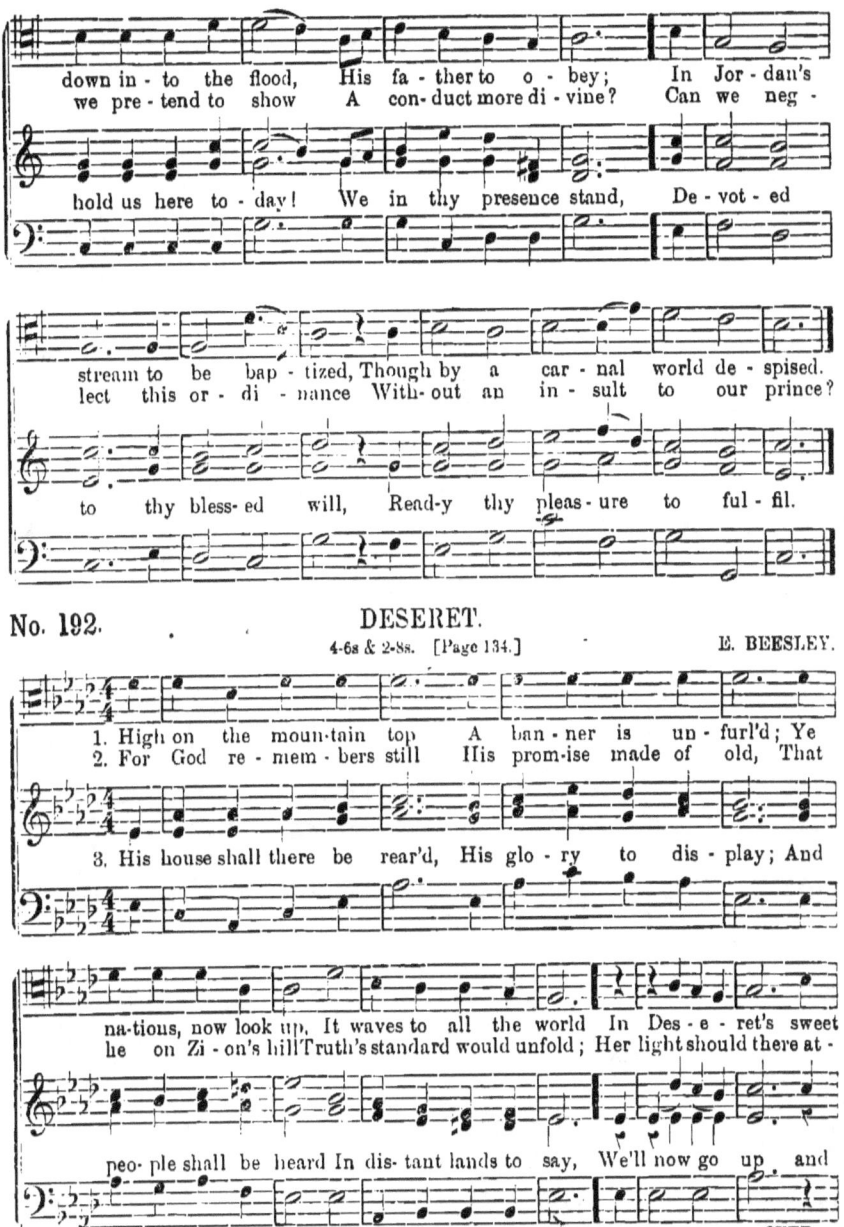

No. 194. GREETING.

4-6s & 2-8s. [Page 346.]

Moderato.   G. CARELESS.

1. All hail! the new-born year! Thrice welcome to the Saints, Whose coming Lord is near, To end their long complaints: Sweet hope, still perching on thy wing, Anticipates a happier spring. Anticipates a happier spring.

2. When life shall spring anew, And vegetation bloom, And flow'rs of varied hue Will spread a rich perfume, While happy birds fill ev'ry grove With songs of joy and life and love. With songs of joy and life and love.

3. These but a type shall be Of glories more sublime; A wondrous Jubilee Hangs on the wings of time; Near and more near redemption comes; Near and more near the sinner's doom. Near and more near the sinner's doom.

4-6s & 2-8s. [Page 12.] G. CARELESS.

1. O happy souls, who pray Where God appoints to hear!
2. No burning heats by day, Nor blasts of ev'ning air,
3. God is the only Lord, Our shield and our defence.

O happy Saints, who pay Their constant service there!
Shall take our health away, If God be with us there.
With gifts his hands are stor'd; We draw our blessings thence.

We'll praise him still, And happy we Who love the way To Zion's hill.
He is our sun, And he our shade To guard the head By night or noon.
He will bestow On Jacob's race Peculiar grace, And glory too.

Who love the way To Zion's hill.
To guard the head By night or noon.
Peculiar grace, And glory too.

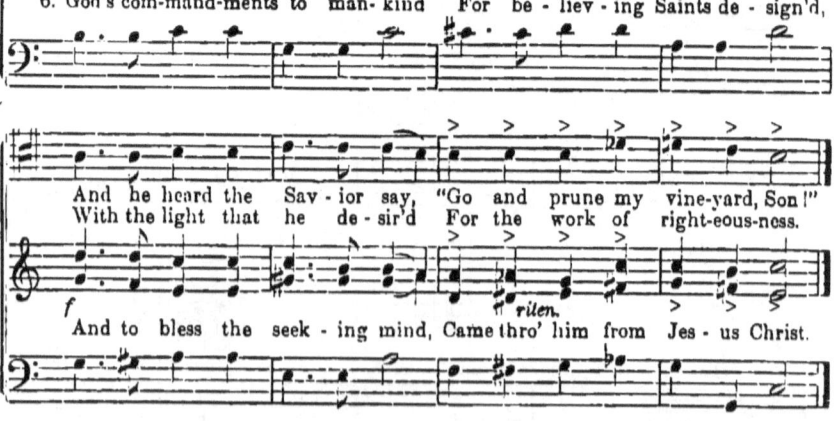

7s. [Page 206.] *English Chorister.*

1. Jes - us, once of hum - ble birth, Now in glo - ry comes to earth; Once he suf - fer'd grief and pain, Now he comes on earth to reign. Now he comes on earth to reign.
2. Once a meek and low - ly lamb, Now the Lord, the great I AM; Once up - on the cross he bowed, Now his char - iot is the cloud. Now his char - iot is the cloud.
3. Once he groan'd in blood and tears, Now in glo - ry he ap - pears; Once re - ject - ed by his own, Now their King he shall be known. Now their King he shall be known.

No. 206. EYRA.
7s. [Page 57.] A. M. FOX

1. Give us room that we may dwell, Zi - on's chil - dren
2. O! how bright the morn - ing seems— Bright - er from so
3. Lo! thy sun goes down no more; God him - self will

8-7s. [Page 63.]

1. Where the voice of friendship's heard, Sounding like a sweet-toned bird;
Where the ho-ly notes in-spire With de-vo-tion's pure de-sire;
Where fond ac-tions speak the soul; Where true love finds no con-trol;
Where the sons of God a-gree, There may all the faith-ful be.

2. Where the wear-y find a home; Where the wild deer fear-less roam;
Where the mel-low fruit-tree grows; Where the gold-en har-vest flows;
Where the bee, the grape and kine Yield their hon-ey, milk and wine;
Where the curse from earth shall flee, There may all the faith-ful be.

3. Where the tem-ple-block is laid; Where no foe shall e'er in-vade;
Where the Priesthood's pow'r shall claim All that heav'n and earth can name;
Where the judge by jus-tice rules; Where the couns'llors are not fools;
Where the poor shall judg-ment see, There may all the faith-ful be.

* The second hymn on page 99 may also be sung to this tune by repeating the 3rd and 4th lines of each verse.

* The hymn on page 148 may also be sung to this tune.

No. 232. **JOYFUL SOUND.**

Cheerfully. 8s & 7s. Double. [Page 38.] E. STEPHENS.

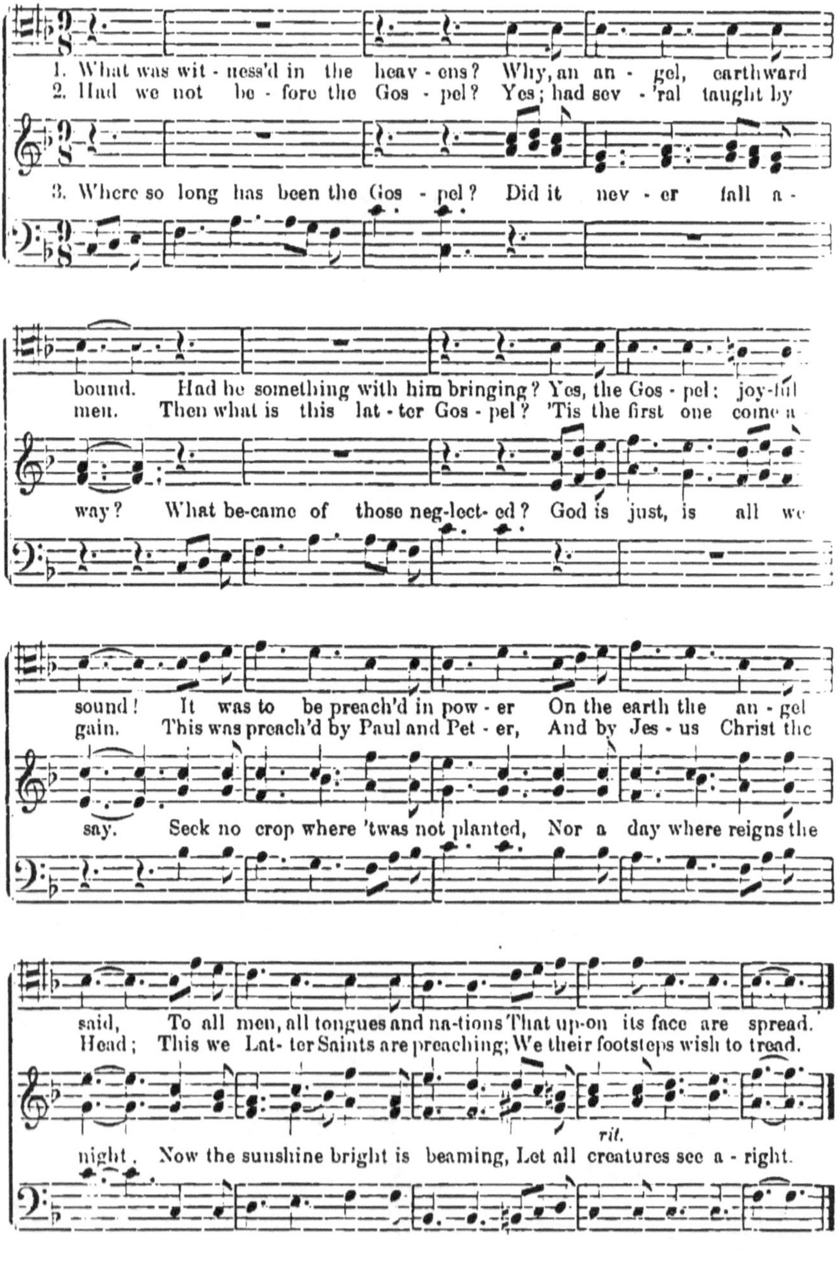

No. 233.   REVELATION.
With feeling.   8s & 7s. Double. [Page 143.]   E. STEPHENS.

1. O my Father, thou that dwell-est In the high and glorious place! When shall I re-gain thy presence, And a-gain be-hold thy face? In thy ho-ly hab-i-ta-tion, Did my spir-it once re-side? In my first pri-me-val child-hood, Was I nurtured near thy side?

2. For a wise and glorious pur-pose Thou hast placed me here on earth, And withhel l the re-col-lec-tion Of my former friends and birth; Yet oft-times a se-cret something Whisper'd, You're a stranger here; And I felt that I had wandered From a more ex-alt-ed sphere.

3. I had learn'd to call thee Father, Through thy Spir-it from on high; But, un-til the Key of Knowledge Was re-stored, I knew not why. In the heav'ns are parents sin-gle? No; the thought makes reason stare! Truth is rea-son; truth e-ter-nal Tells me, I've a moth-er there.

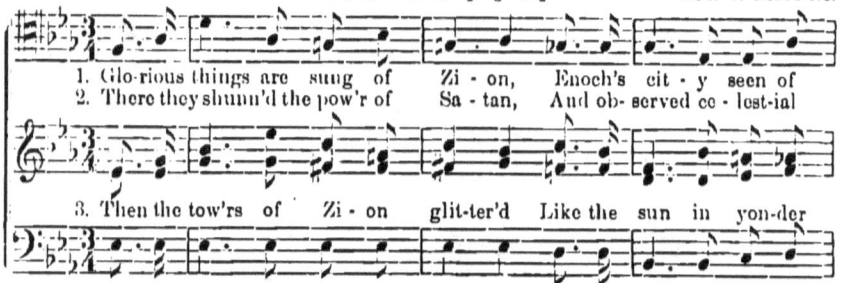
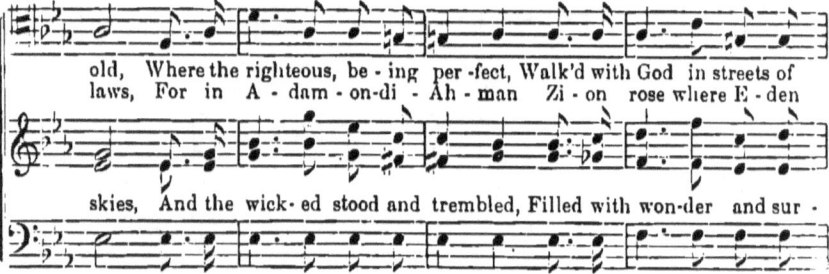
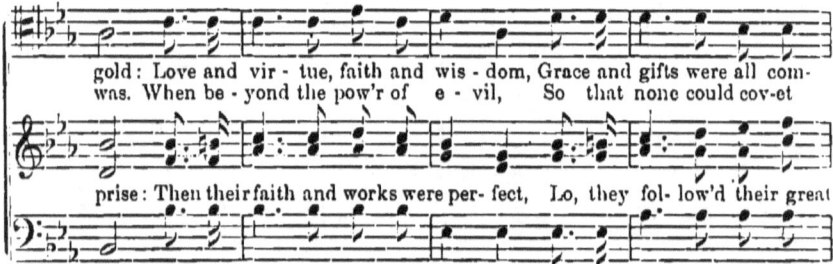
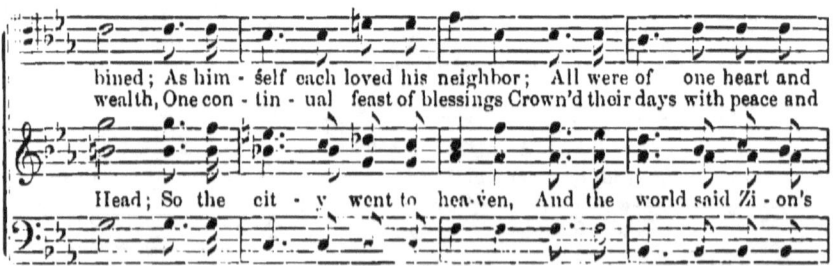

8s, 7s & 4. [Page 259.] ANNIE F. HARRISON.

1. Guide us, O Thou great Je-ho-vah, Saints un-to the promised land!
2. Op-en, Jes-us, Zi-on's fountains, Let her rich-est blessings come,
3. When the earth be-gins to trem-ble, Bid our fear-ful thoughts be still;

We are weak, but Thou art a-ble, Hold us with thy pow'r-ful hand.
Let the fier-y, cloud-y pil-lar Guard us to this ho-ly home.
When thy judgments spread de-struc-tion, Keep us safe on Zi-on's hill.

Ho-ly Spir-it, Ho-ly Spir-it, Feed us till the Sav-ior comes.
Great Re-deemer, Great Re-deem-er, Bring, O, bring the wel-come day!

Sing-ing prais-es, Sing-ing prais-es, Songs of glo-ry un-to thee.

Ho-ly Spir-it, Ho-ly Spir-it, Feed us till the Sav-ior comes.
Great Re-deem-er, Great Re-deem-er, Bring, O, bring the wel-come day!

Sing-ing prais-es, Sing-ing prais-es, Songs of glo-ry un-to thee.

* The hymn on page 143 may also be sung to this tune.

No. 238. GATHERING.*
8s, 7s & 4. [Page 154.]
T. C. GRIGGS

1. Israel, Israel, God is calling; Calling thee from lands of woe;
2. Israel, Israel, God is speaking; Hear your great De-liv'-rers voice!
3. Israel, angels are de-scend-ing From ce-les-tial worlds on high,

Ba-by-lon the great is fall-ing God shall all her towers oer-throw.
Now a glorious morn is break-ing For the peo-ple of his choice.
And towards man their powers extending, That the Saints may homeward fly.

Come to Zi-on, Come to Zi-on E'er His floods of an-ger flow.
Come to Zi-on, Come to Zi-on And with-in her walls re-joice.
Come to Zi-on, Come to Zi-on, For your coming Lord is nigh.

*The hymn on page 94. may also be sung to this tune.

No. 239. HERALD.
8s, 7s & s. [Page 95.]
H. H. PETERSEN

1. O'er the gloomy hills of darkness, Look, my soul, be still and gaze;
2. Let the Indian and the Negro, Let the rude Bar-bar-ian see
3. Kingdoms wide that sit in darkness, Grant them Lord the glorious light,

SAFETY. [Concluded]

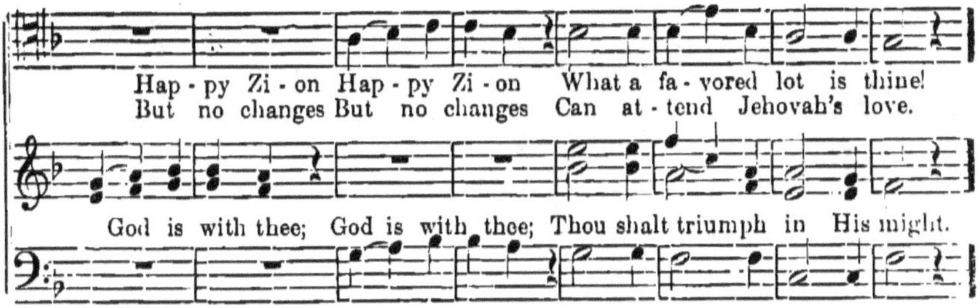

Hap-py Zi-on Hap-py Zi-on What a fa-vored lot is thine!
But no changes But no changes Can at-tend Jehovah's love.

God is with thee; God is with thee; Thou shalt triumph in His might.

No. 245.   EDGEWARE.
8s, [Page 281.]
J. I. COBBIN.

1. When Joseph his brethren be-held Afflict-ed and trembling with
2. A-while his behavior was rough, To bring their past sins to their
3. How little they thought it was he, Whom they had ill treated and

fear, Afflicted and trembling with fear His heart with compassion was
mind, To bring their past sins to their mind, But when they were humbled e-
sold! Whom they had ill treated and sold! How great their confusion must

fill'd From weeping he could not forbear. From weeping he could not forbear
nough He hastened to show himself kind. He hastened to show himself kind.
be,   As soon as his name he had told! As soon as his name he had told.

WOOBURN. (Concluded.)

No. 250.

DIMICK.*
7s, & 6s. [Page 342.]

1. O, stop and tell me, Red Man, Who are you, why you roam, And how you get your living; Have you no God, no home? 2. With stature straight and portly, And decked in native pride, With feathers, paints and brooches, He willingly replied:

3. "I once was pleasant Ephraim. When Jacob for me prayed, But O, how blessings vanish, When man from God has strayed! 4. Before your nation knew us, Some thousand moons ago, Our fathers fell in darkness, And wander'd to and fro.

5. And long they've lived by hunting Instead of work and arts, And so our race has dwindled To idle Indian hearts. 6. Yet hope within us lingers, As if the Spirit spoke, He'll come for your redemption, And break your Gentile yoke.

*The Hymn on page 257 may also be sung to this tune.

No. 253. MORGAN.
7s & 6s, Double. [Page 210.] T. C. GRIGGS.

1. Fare-well, all earth-ly hon-ors, I bid you all a-dieu; Fare-well, all sin-ful pleasures, I want no more of you. I want my hab-i-ta-tion On that e-ter-nal soil, Be-yond the pow'rs of Sa-tan, Where sin can ne'er de-file.

2. I want my name en-grav-en A-mong the righteous ones, Crying ho-ly, ho-ly Fath-er, And wear a right-eous crown. For such e-ter-nal rich-es I'm will-ing to pass through All need-ful tri-bu-la-tions, And count them my just due.

3. I'm will-ing to be chastened, And bear my dai-ly cross; I'm will-ing to be cleansed From ev-'ry kind of dross. I see a fier-y fur-nace, I feel its piercing flame; The fruits of it are ho-ly, The gold will still re-main.

rit.

SWEET REST.

(Concluded).

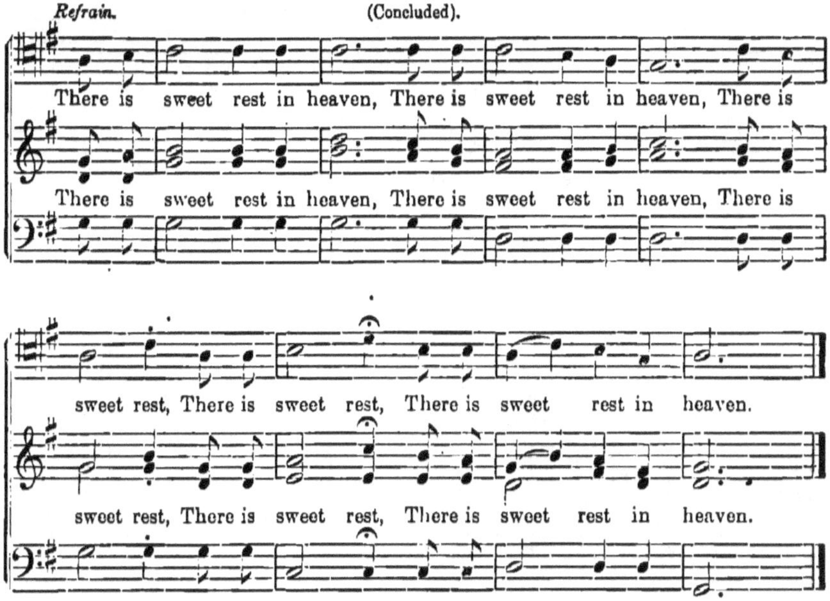
Refrain.
There is sweet rest in heaven, There is sweet rest in heaven, There is
There is sweet rest in heaven, There is sweet rest in heaven, There is
sweet rest, There is sweet rest, There is sweet rest in heaven.
sweet rest, There is sweet rest, There is sweet rest in heaven.

No. 257.

SAMOA.

7s & 6s, [Page 234.]

G. CARELESS.

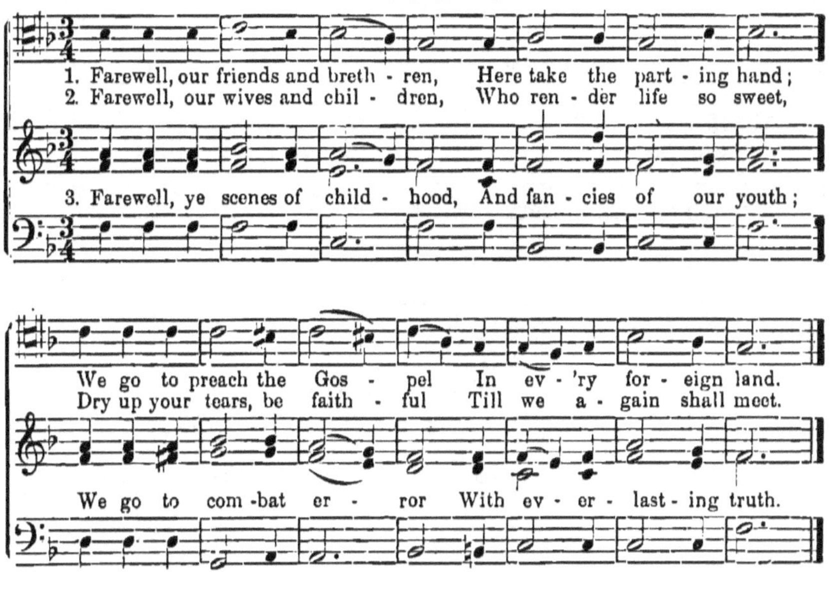
1. Farewell, our friends and breth - ren, Here take the part - ing hand;
2. Farewell, our wives and chil - dren, Who ren - der life so sweet,
3. Farewell, ye scenes of child - hood, And fan - cies of our youth;
We go to preach the Gos - pel In ev - 'ry for - eign land.
Dry up your tears, be faith - ful Till we a - gain shall meet.
We go to com -bat er - ror With ev - er - last - ing truth.

7s. & 6s. [Page 257.] JOHN TULLIDGE.

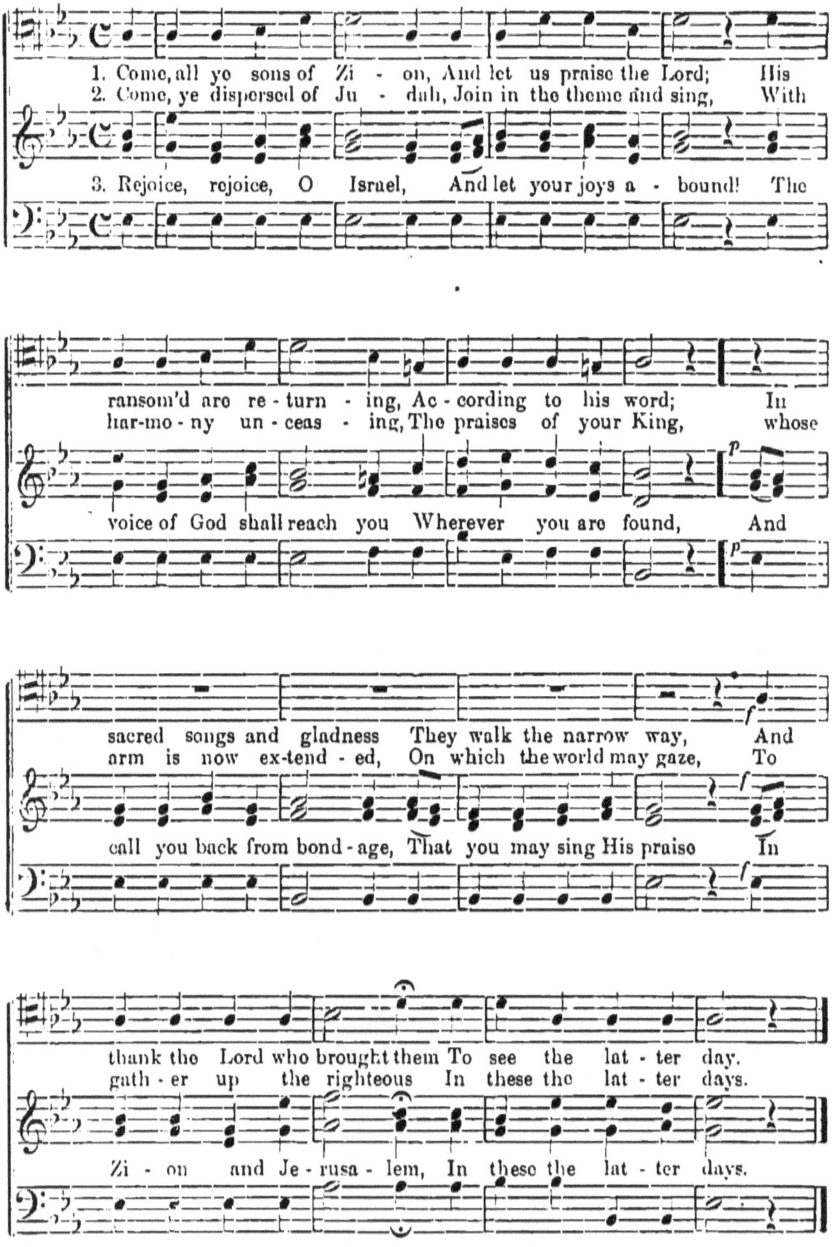

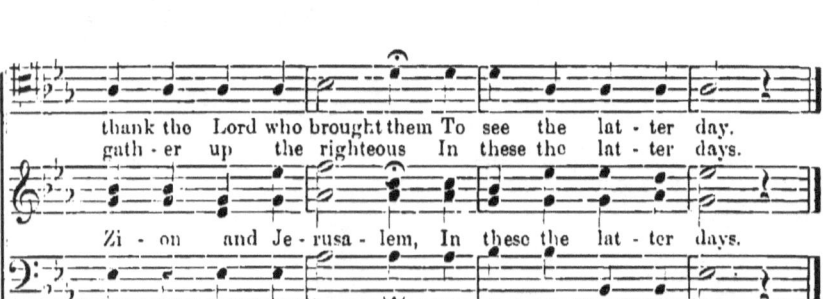

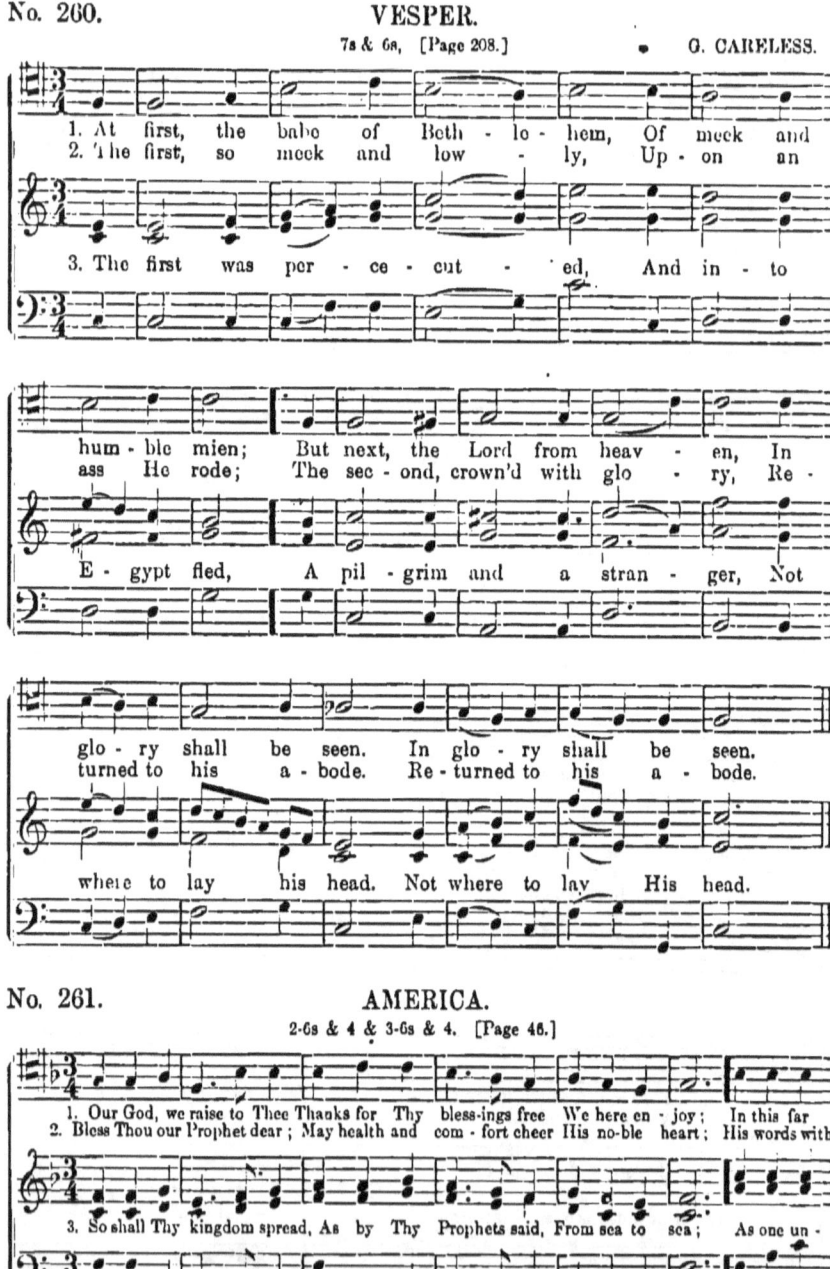

No. 263. **GLORY.**

8-8-6s. [Page 36.] A. RADIGER.

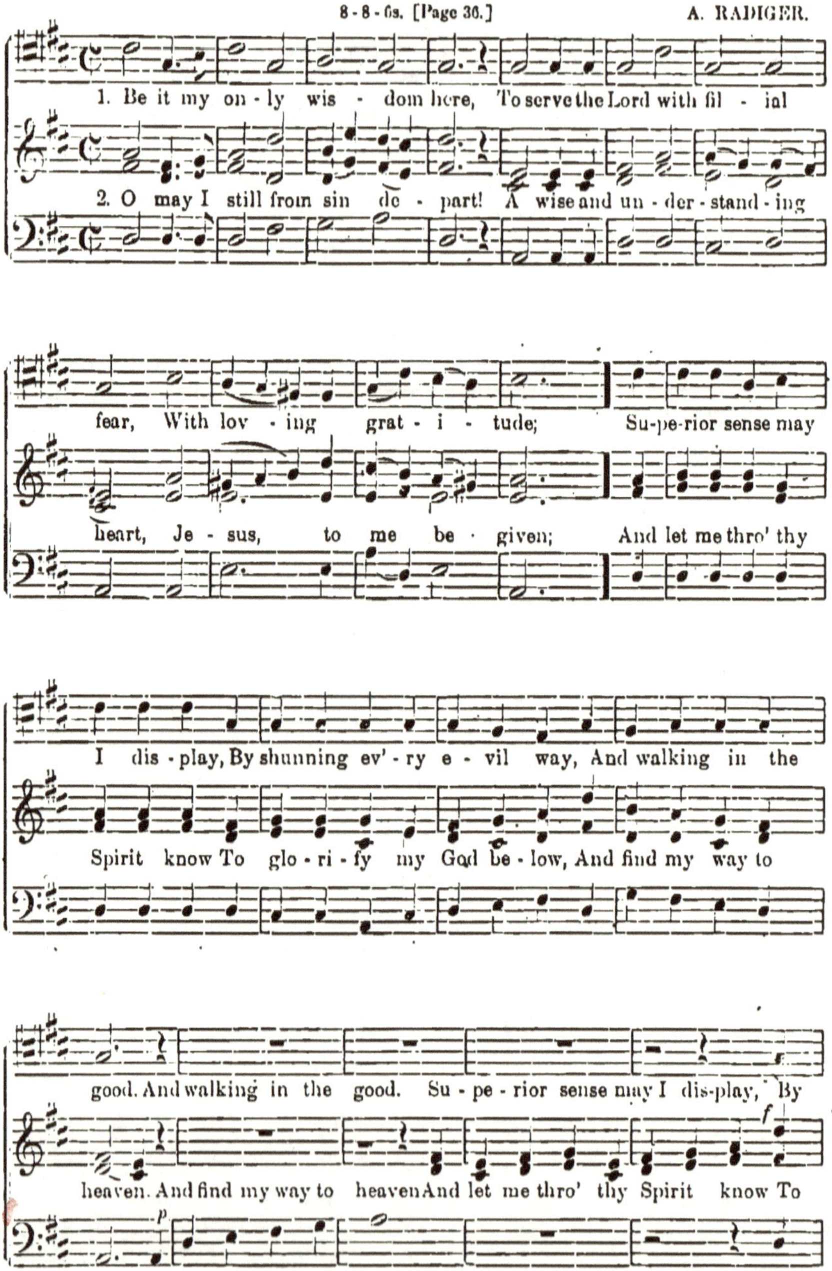

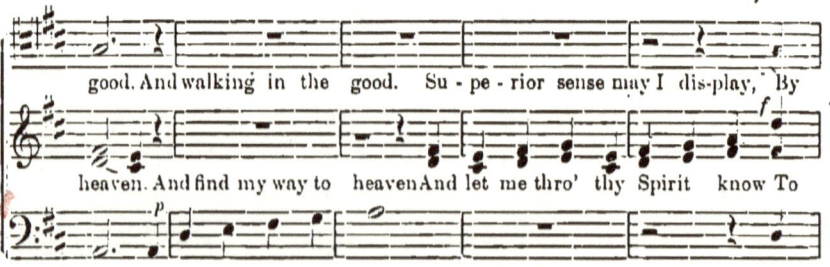

No. 268. WEBER. JOS. J. DAYNES.
2-8s & 6. [Page 123.]

1. Come, let us pur-pose with one heart To fol-low vir-tue,
2. With dil-i-gence we'll still pur-sue Those acts of grace and
3. Neat in our dress, not sump-tuous clad, Nor vain, nor som-bre—

and im-part The bliss of life be-low— That we in-
mer-cy due To toil-worn, lab-'ring men! We'll aid the
look-ing sad, In all our gar-ments clean! Fresh in our

dus-trious-ly may live, And by our la-bor have to give, As
help-less and se-cure The means of life to help the poor, And
bod-ies, whole our clothes, And free from all the Spir-it loathes, Nor

Gos-pel pre-cepts show... As Gos-pel pre-cepts show.
help them all we can... And help them all we can.
proud, nor low-ly mean... Nor proud, nor low-ly mean.

No. 269.   BALLO.
Tempo di Marcia. 9s & 8s. [Page 393.]   JOHN TULLIDGE.

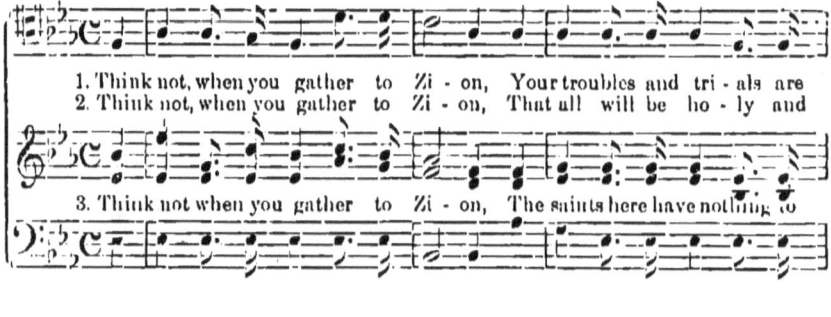

1. Think not, when you gather to Zi-on, Your troubles and tri-als are
2. Think not, when you gather to Zi-on, That all will be ho-ly and
3. Think not when you gather to Zi-on, The saints here have nothing to

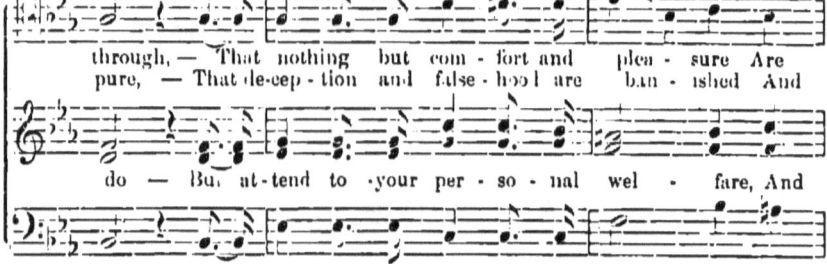

through,— That nothing but com-fort and plea-sure Are
pure,— That de-cep-tion and false-hood are ban-ished And
do — But at-tend to your per-so-nal wel-fare, And

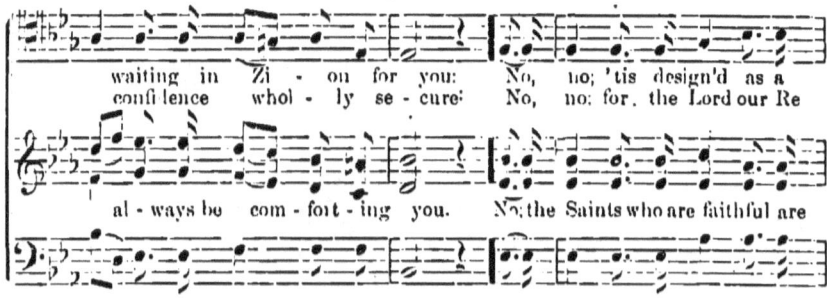

waiting in Zi-on for you: No, no; 'tis design'd as a
confidence whol-ly se-cure: No, no: for the Lord our Re-
al-ways be com-fort-ing you. No, the Saints who are faithful are

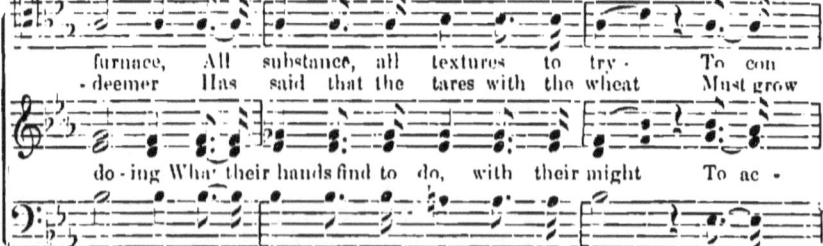

furnace, All substance, all textures to try. To con-
deemer Has said that the tares with the wheat Must grow
doing Wha' their hands find to do, with their might To ac-

FOWLER.
(Concluded.)

bless - ing Be - stowed by thy boun - te - ous hand; We
good - ness, We've proved him in days that are past; The

fec - tion The hon - est and faith - ful will go; While

feel it a plea-sure to serve thee, And love to o - bey thy commands.
wicked who fight a- gainst Zi - on Will sure-ly be smit- ten at last.

they who re - ject the glad mes- sage, Shall nev - er such hap-pi - ness know.

No. 272.   PENROSE.
9s & 8s, [Page 73.]

1. Up, a - wake, ye de - fend - ers of Zi - on! The
2. By the moun - tains our Zi - on's sur - rounded; Her

3. Shall we bear with op - pres - sion for ev - er? Shall we

foe's at the door of your homes; Let each heart be the heart of a
warriors are no - ble and brave; And their faith on Je - ho - vah is

tame- ly sub - mit to the foe, While the ties of our kind - red they

PENROSE.
(Continued.)

ASSEMBLY.
(Concluded.)

lat - ter day glo - ry be - gins to come forth, We'll sing and we'll
an - gels are com - ing to vis - it the earth.
stor - ing their judg - es and all as at first; We'll sing and we'll
vail o'er the earth is be - gin - ing to burst.

shout with the ar - mies of heav - en Ho - san - na, ho-
shout with the ar - mies of heav - en, Ho - san - na, ho-

san - na to God and the lamb! Let glo - ry to them in the
san - na to God and the lamb! Let glo - ry to them in the

high - est be giv - en, Hence-forth and for - ev - er a - men and a - men.
high - est be giv - en, Hence-forth and for - ev - er a - men and a - men.

* The hymn on page 190 may also be sung to this tune.

ELSINORE.
(Concluded.)

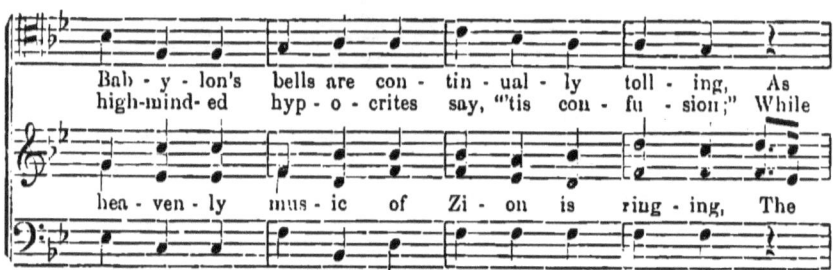

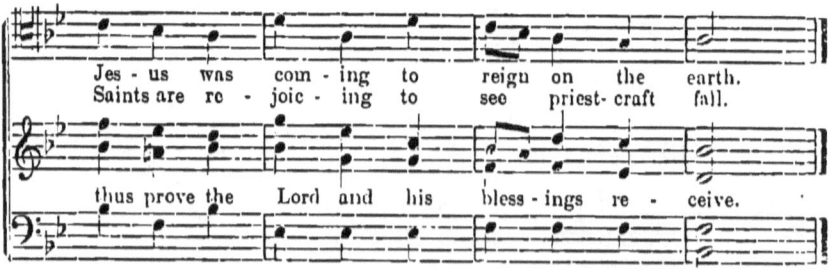

No. 276. PHELPS.
12s & 11s. [Page 198.]

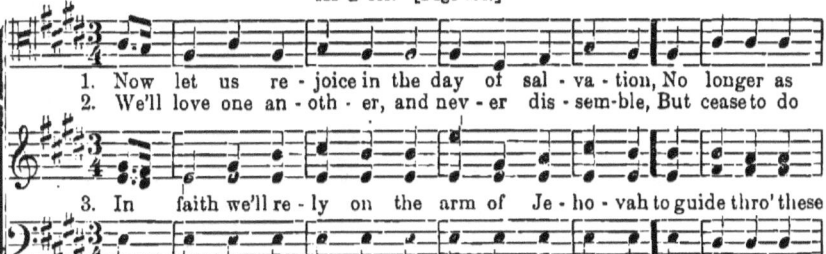

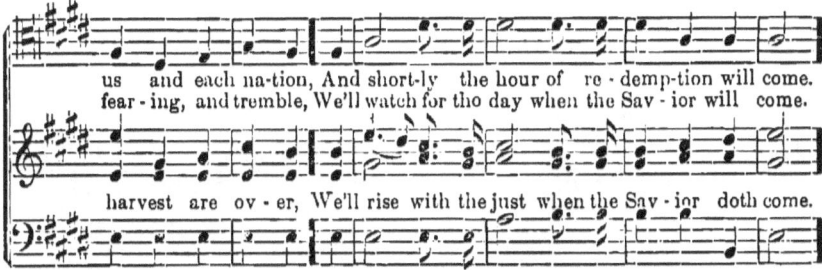
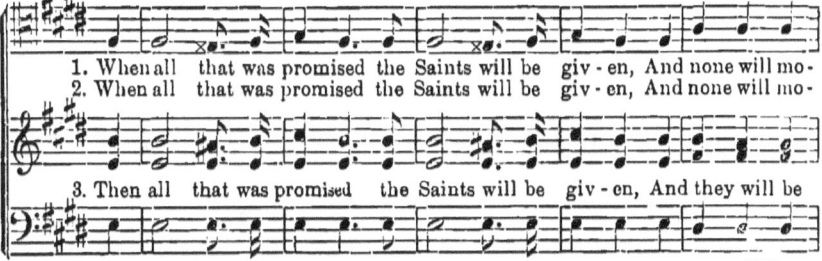

over.

VIVA.
(Continued.)

VIVA.
(Concluded.)

laughed thee to scorn; Thou naught but af-flic-tion and sor-row hast
deem - er and friend, To cheer thee, and bless thee, and dry up thy

bow down to thee; Ten men shall take hold of the skirt of the

seen; Heart - rend-ing and cheer-less thy path-way has been.
tears, And calm the sad bo - som, and chase all thy fears.

Jew, And say, "With you we'll go, for Je - ho - vah's with you.

No. 280. WYNONA.
10s. [Page 371.] MENDELSSOHN.

1. "Great Spir-it! list - en to the red man's wail! Thou hast the
3. "With curs'd fire-wat - ers stu-pe-fy-ing flame, (Which lull'd the

5. "And shall our na - tion, once so great de - cay? Our children

pow'r to help him in his woe, Thy mighty arm was nev-er known to
sens - es of our chiefs to rest,) Soft-mouthed words, the cheating pale-face

per - ish, and our chieftains die? Great Spir-it, help!—thy glo-rious pow'r dis-

* The hymn on page 361. may also be sung to this tune.

No. 282.   FIDELITY.
11s, [Page 260.]

No. 285. LEONE. L. D. EDWARDS.
11s. [Page 351.]

1. O thou who has promised in love to receive The children of those who in Jesus believe, Thy Spirit impart and our bosoms inspire, And seal them thine own with thine unction and fire.
2. Receive them, our Father, as lambs that were lost; The blood of thy Son is the price they have cost. By the pow'r of the Priesthood, thy blessings bestow On those to thy service we dedicate now.
3. Let thy mercy surround them, thou Father adored, To obey the commands of our crucified Lord; Thy Spirit forever their goodness has giv'n, We bless them as thine in the kingdom of heav'n.

No. 286. SWEET HOME.
Andante. 11s. [Page 318.]

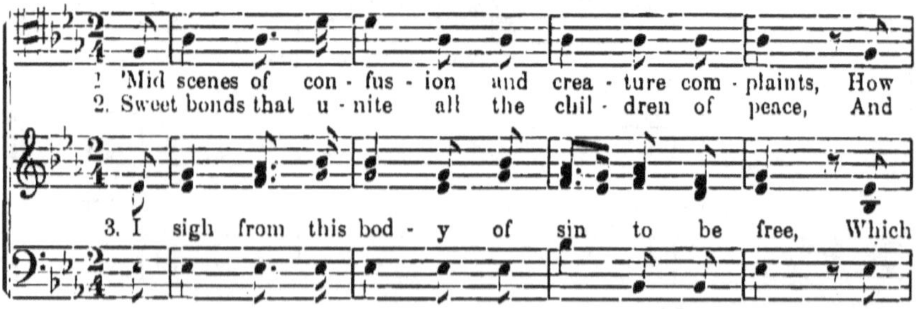

1. 'Mid scenes of confusion and creature complaints, How
2. Sweet bonds that unite all the children of peace, And
3. I sigh from this body of sin to be free, Which

SWEET HOME.
(Concluded.)

ALPINE.
(Concluded.)

No. 300. ADAM.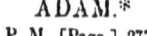
P. M. [Page] 277.

1. This earth was once a gar-den place, With all her glo-ries com-mon; And men did live a ho-ly race, And worship Je-sus face to face, In Adam-on-di Ah-man.
2. We read that E-noch walked with God, A-bove the power of Mam-mon; While Zi-on spread her-self a-broad, And Saints and an-gels sang a-loud, In Adam-on-di Ah-man.
3. Her land was good and great-ly blest, Be-yond old Is-rael's ca-naan; Her fame was known from east to west, Her peace was great and pure the rest Of Adam-on-di Ah-man.

* The hymn on page 206 may also be sung to this tune.

No. 301. CALDWELL.
P. M. [Page 273.]

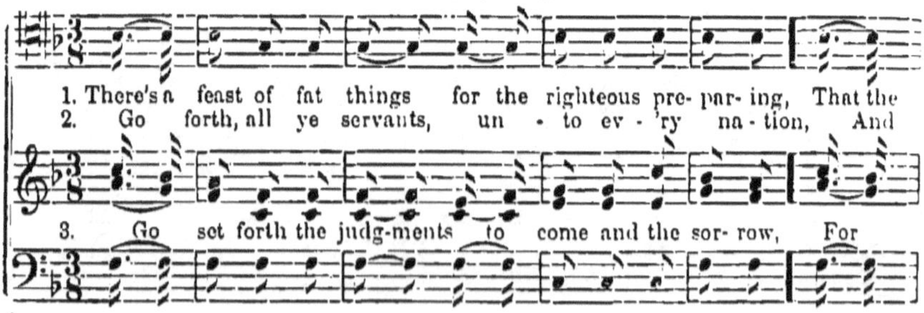

1. There's a feast of fat things for the righteous pre-par-ing, That the
2. Go forth, all ye servants, un-to ev-'ry na-tion, And
3. Go set forth the judg-ments to come and the sor-row, For

CALDWELL.
(Concluded.)

good of this world all the Saints may be sharing; For the harvest is
lift up your voices and make proc‑la‑ma‑tion. To cease from all

aft‑er to day. oh! there cometh to‑morrow, When the wick‑ed, un‑

ripe and the reapers have learned To gather the wheat that the
e‑vil and leave off all mirth, For the Sav‑ior is com‑ing to

godly, re‑bell‑ious and proud, Shall be burned up as stubble—oh,

Rit *Cho.*

tares may be burned. Come to the sup‑per, come to the
reign on the earth.

cry it a‑loud. Come to the sup‑per come to the

sup‑per, Come to the sup‑per of the great Bride‑groom.

sup‑per, Come to the sup‑per of the great Bride‑groom.

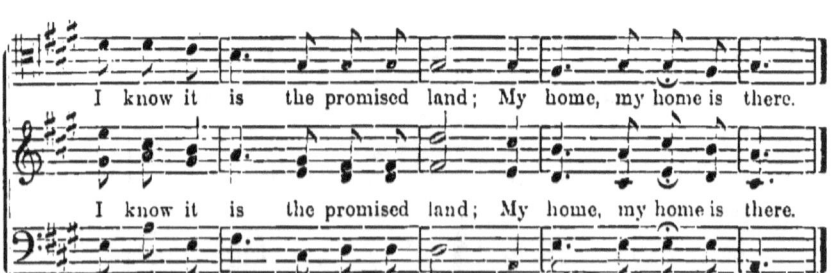

No. 303. CLAYTON.
P. M. [Page 390.]

over.

DAWNING.
(Concluded.)

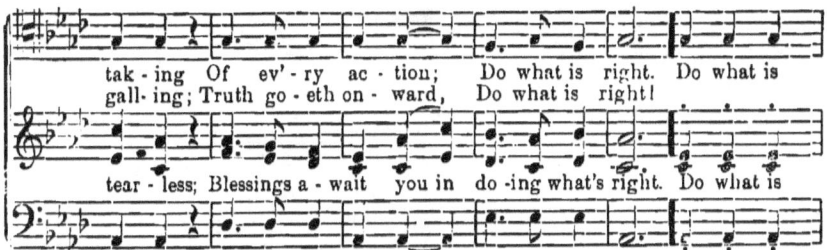

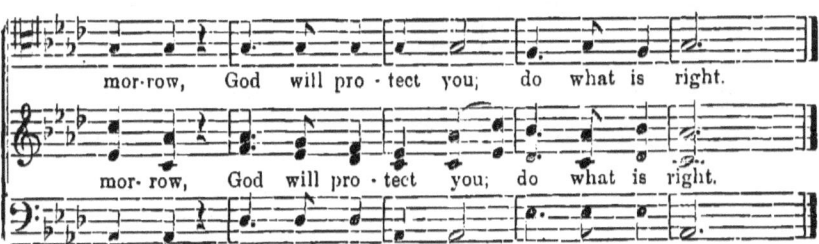

*The hymn on page 191 may also be sung to this tune.

No. 312.

JAQUES.
P. M. [Page 71.]

1. O say what is truth: 'Tis the fair-est gem That the rich-es of worlds can pro-duce; And price-less the val-ue of truth will be when The proud mon-arch's cost-li-est di-a-dem Is count-ed but dross and re-fuse.

2. Yes, say what is truth? 'Tis the bright-est prize To which mor-tals or Gods can as-pire: Go search in the depths where it glit-ter-ing lies, Or as-cend in pur-suit to the lof-ti-est skies, 'Tis an aim for the no-blest de-sire.

3. The scep-tre may fall from the des-pot's grasp When with winds of stern jus-tice he copes, But the pil-lar of truth will en-dure to the last, And its firm-root-ed bul-warks out-stand the rude blast, And the wreck of the fell ty-rant's hopes.

JOSHUA.
(Concluded.)

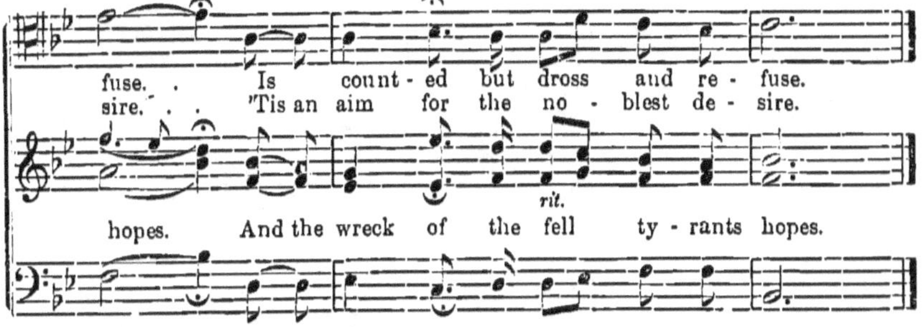

fuse. . Is count-ed but dross and re-fuse.
sire. . 'Tis an aim for the no-blest de-sire.
hopes. And the wreck of the fell ty-rants hopes.

No. 314.   **JOSEPH THE SEER.**
P. M. (Page 337.)   SOLO.   NEUKOMM.
                                                                   Arr. by E. Beesley.
Allegro moderato.

1. The Seer, the Seer, Jos-eph the Seer! I'll sing of the Prophet
2. The Saints, the Saints, his ho-ly pride, For them he lived, for

ev-er dear! the Pro-phet ev-er dear!
them he died! he lived, for them he died!

His e-qual now can-not be found, By search-ing
Their joys were his, their sor-rows too; He loved the

over.

JOSEPH THE SEER.
(Continued.)

tho wide world a-round. With Gods he
Saints— he loved Nau-voo. Un-changed in

CHORUS.

soared in the realms of day, And men he taught the
death, with a Sav-ior's love, He pleads their cause in the

heav'n-ly way, And men he taught the heav'n-ly way. The
courts a-bove. He pleads tneir cause in the courts a-bove. The

earth-ly Seer! the heav'n-ly Seer! I love to dwell on his
Seer, the Seer! Jos-eph the Seer! O, how I love his

JOSEPH THE SEER.
(Concluded.)

mem-or-y dear: The chosen of God and the friend of man, He brought the
mem-or-y dear! The just and wise the pure and free, A fa-ther he

SOLO.

Priesthood back a-gain; He gazed on the past, on the
was and is to me. Let fiends now rage in

pres - ent too, And opened And opened the heav'nly world to
their dark hour— No matter, No matter, he is beyond their

CHORUS.

view. And opened And opened the heav'n-ly world to view.
power. No matter, No matter, he is be-yond their power.

No. 315. LIBERTY.
P. M. (Page 376.)

1. O! ye moun-tains high, where the clear blue sky Arch-es o-ver the vales of the free, Where the pure breezes blow And the clear streamlets flow, How I've longed to your bosom to flee. O Zi-on! dear Zion! home of the free; My own mountain home now to

2. Though the great and the wise all thy beau-ties des-pise, To the humble and pure thou art dear: Though the haughty may smile, And the wick-ed re-vile, Yet we love thy glad tidings to hear. O Zi-on! dear Zion! home of the free; Though thou wert forced to fly to thy

3. In thy mountain re-treat, God will strengthen thy feet; On the necks of thy foes thou shalt tread, And their sil-ver and gold, as the Prophets have told, Shall be brought to a-dorn thy fair head. O Zi-on! dear Zion! home of the free; Soon thy tow-ers will shine with a

NAISBITT.
(Continued.)

NAISBITT.

(Concluded.)

east to west- ern sea, And march thro' the earth, vic - to - ri - ous!
east to west- ern sea, And march thro' the earth, vic - to - ri - ous!

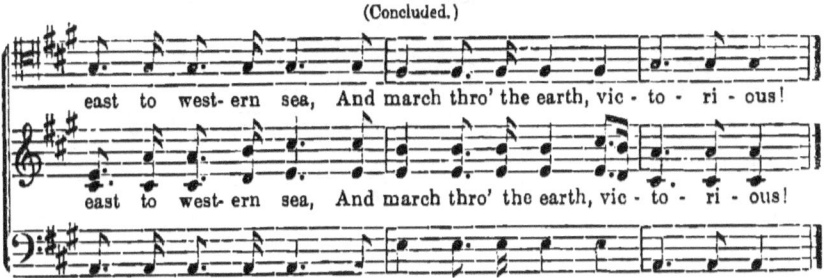

No. 319.

NEW SALEM.*

P. M. (Page 212.)

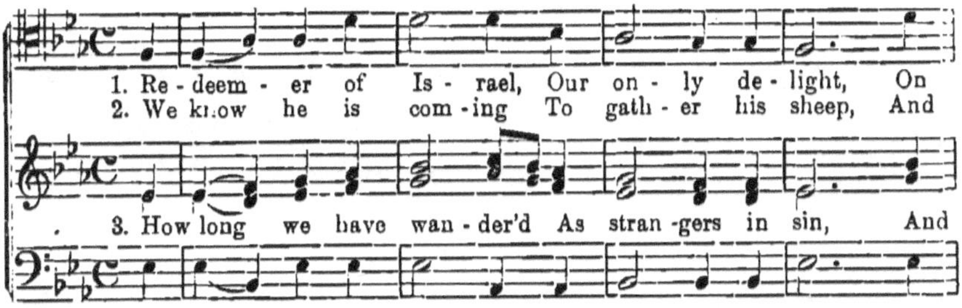
1. Re - deem - er of Is - rael, Our on - ly de - light, On
2. We know he is com - ing To gath - er his sheep, And
3. How long we have wan - der'd As stran - gers in sin, And

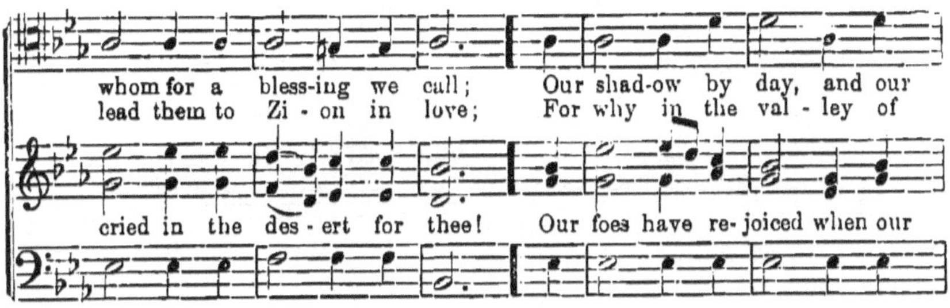
whom for a bless-ing we call; Our shad-ow by day, and our
lead them to Zi - on in love; For why in the val - ley of
cried in the des - ert for thee! Our foes have re - joiced when our

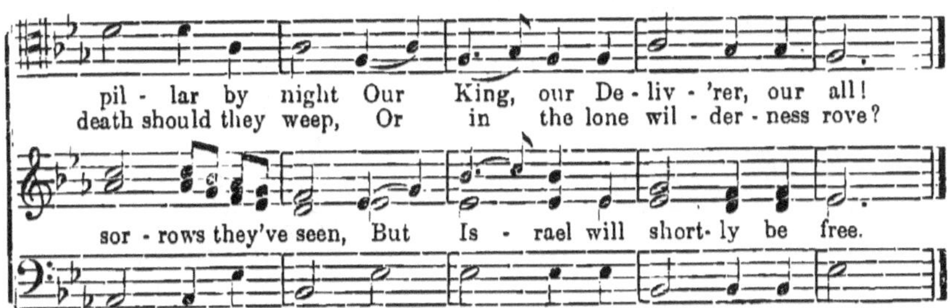
pil - lar by night Our King, our De - liv - 'rer, our all!
death should they weep, Or in the lone wil - der - ness rove?
sor - rows they've seen, But Is - rael will short- ly be free.

* The hymn on page 307 may also be sung to this tune.

* The hymn on page 352 may also be sung to this tune.

PALMER.
(Concluded.)

Oh, that's the God for me! Oh, that's the God for me!
Oh, that's the Church for me! Oh, that's the Church for me!

Oh, that's the Church for me. Oh, that's the Church for me.

No. 321. ## PARADISE.
Moderato. P. M. [Page 335.] AUBER.

1. Weep, weep not for me, Zi - on; Re - joice now and sing ye a-
2. To smite with a rod of his pow - er, To lay Zion's en - e - mies
3. Long, long, dear Saints, we have wan - der'd, Yet, yet we will not com-

loud; Pray, pray that Ju - dah's fierce li - on May quickly des-
low; While frowns on his coun-ten - ance low - er, They sink to per-
plain; Though oft our all has been plun - dered, The loss is our

cend in a cloud: Haste, haste; haste, haste; oh, quickly des-cend in a cloud.
di - tion and woe: Yes, yes, yes, yes, they sink to per - di - tion and woe.
in - fin - ite gain: Yes, yes, yes, yes, the loss is our in - fin - ite gain.

PRESTON.
(Concluded.)

CHORUS. Moderato.

A-rise! for the time has come, Is-rael must gath-er home, High on the
Sound the a-larm of war, Thro' nations near and far, Let its dread

Come, let us haste a-way, Here we'll no long-er stay; Zi-on, thy

mountains the En-sign we see; Fall'n is the Gen-tile power,
tones be heard o'er land and sea. Zi-on shall dwell in peace,

beauties we're yearn-ing to see. Saints raise the heav'nly song,

Soon will their reign be o'er, Tyrants must rule no more, Is-rael Israel is free!
Is-rael will still in-crease, Lib-er-ty ne'er shall se, Is-rael Israel is free!

Join with the ransom'd throng, Angel's the notes pro-long, Is-rael Israel is free!

No. 324. PATTEN.
6s & 7s. D. (Page 194.)

1. Let us pray, glad-ly pray, In the house of Je-ho-vah, Till the
2. What a joy will be there, At the great re-sur-rec-tion, As the

3. We can then live in peace, With a joy on the mountains, As the

RALLY.
(Concluded.)

No. 328.   WILLES.
SOLO.   P. M. [Page 381.]   Arr. by E. BEESLEY.

1. There is a place in U-tah, that I re-mem-ber well, And
2. When wintry winds are storm-ing, and snow is fall-ing deep, Then
3. The storm-king has no ter-rors when wintry winds blow cold; We

there the Saints in peace and joy and plen-ty ev-er dwell; My
rich supplies are form-ing a-mong the mountains steep; The
light-en all life's sor-rows in our love-ly Mountain Fold; We

Mountain Home, thou'rt dear to me! to thee I fond-ly cling,— While
fer-til-i-sing crys-tal streams, when sun-ny skies il-lume, Make
wor-ship there; we dance and sing a-mong the joy-ful throng, And

here I roam, far from my home, my Mountain Home I sing.
Na-ture's ver-dant bo-som teem with-in my Mountain Home.
there our tithes and off'rings bring, which to the Lord be-long.

over.

L. M. or 6-8s. (Page 277.) MOZART.

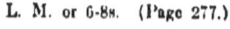

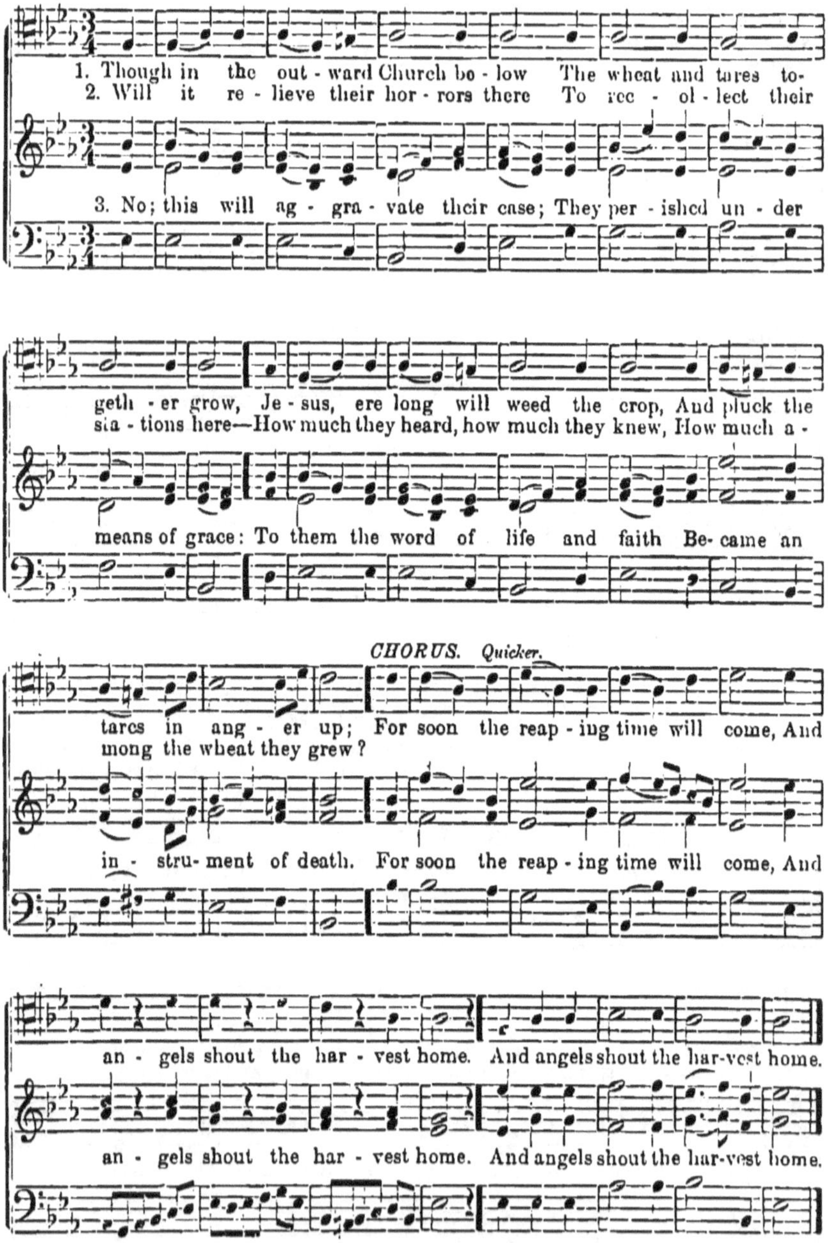

GENERAL INDEX OF TUNES.

Name	No.	Name	No.	Name	No.
Abram	7	Communion	20	Good Tidings	123
Acacia	201	Compassion	190	Goshen	283
Ada	208	Confidence	177	Gospel	237
Adam	300	Confirmation	110	Gospel Light	217
Adieu	235	Contrition	112	Grace	179
Adina	249	Courage	105	Grantsville	311
Adoption	163	Covenant	189	Gratitude	124
Adora	214	Cowper	107	Gray	292
Adoration	4	Creation	113	Greeting	194
Advent	3	Cumorah	187	Hannah	126
Agnes	174	Davenport	305	Harmony	35
Albion	6	David	216	Harold	125
Alfred	12	Dawning	304	Hartford	130
Alicia	99	Dedication	116	Harvest	31
Alman	8	Deliverance	205	Heavenly Home	37
Aloha	10	Deseret	192	Heber	32
Alpha	175	Devotion	22	Herald	239
Alpine	299	Dimick	250	Home	129
America	261	Divinity	191	Hope	127
Amphion	248	Dorcas	115	Horace	128
Animation	1	Downham	114	Hosanna	36
Antigua	11			Hudson	33
Appleton	5	Ebenezer	117	Humanity	218
Arion	9	Eden	24	Hyrum	34
Arizona	100	Edgeware	245		
Ascription	209	Edwinston	25	Immanuel	40
Assembly	274	Elijah	251	Incarnation	131
Assurance	2	Eliza R.	165	Inspiration	91
Atlantic	101	Elliot	330	Invitation	240
Atonement	173	Elsinore	275	Invocation	132
Azalia	202	Emery	23	Irene	39
		Enoch	118	Israel	38
Babylon	281	Erastus	307		
Ballo	269	Eternity	26	Jacob	41
Bedford	103	Eucharist	88	Jaques	312
Benediction	102	Eva	270	Java	42
Bellienall	296	Evan	306	Jeanette	44
Benson	203	Eyra	206	Jed	219
Bereavement	17	Ezra	308	Jonathan	43
Bethlehem	13			Jordan	93
Beulah	16	Faith	27	Joseph	45
Bishop	176	Farewell	166	Joseph the Seer	314
Blessing	164	Far West	309	Joshua	313
Bountiful	215	Felicity	193	Joyful Sound	232
Bradford	15	Festival	122	Judah	92
Brentford	14	Fidelity	282	Justice	98
Brigham	18	Finsley	211		
Brightness	277	Flora	207	Kimball	47
Bryant	19	Forgiveness	119	Kindness	46
Burton	210	Fortitude	120	Kirtland	298
		Fowler	271	Kolob	252
Caldwell	301	Freedom	28		
Caleb	204	Friendship	121	Lamentation	329
Calvary	111			Laura	220
Carthage	89	Gabriel	30	Lavinia	133
Cannon	106	Gardner	178	Lehi	49
Cecil	104	Gathering	238	Leone	285
Celebration	188	Georgia	212	Liberty	315
Charity	109	Gethsemane	29	Light Divine	48
Cheltenham	302	Gladness	195	Lowell	50
China	21	Glendale	310	Lucas	316
Chorister	108	Gloaming	236	Lyman	284
Clayton	303	Glory	263	Lyon	167
Comfort	90				

GENERAL INDEX OF TUNES.

Name	No.	Name	No.	Name	No.
Maggie	137	Promise	146	Strength	78
Majesty	168	Protection	95	Supplication	255
Malachi	55	Providence	96	Sweet Home	286
Manti	264			Sweet Rest	256
Martha	186	Quebec	149		
Marion	289	Quietude	63	Tamar	228
Martyr	278	Quincy	242	Tancie	246
Meditation	51			Taylor	81
Melody	54	Rachael	222	Teasdale	258
Memory	52	Rapture	196	Temple	273
Memorium	135	Rally	325	Testimony	213
Mercy	138	Raymond	223	Thatcher	156
Michael	317	Redeemer	66	Transport	229
Minstrel	221	Redemption	67	Tribute	157
Missionary	169	Reflection	97	Trinity	155
Morgan	253	Reliance	69	Triumph	198
Mormon	136	Relief	68	Truth	80
Mother	53	Repose	297		
Mt. Zion	134	Rest	266	Unity	184
		Restoration	64	Union	158
Naisbitt	318	Resurrection	150	Ure	295
New Hope	265	Reunion	181	Utopia	172
Nephi	141	Revelation	233		
New Salem	319	Reverence	65	Veneration	159
New Year	140	Roxie	294	Vernon	82
Norway	139	Russell	151	Vesper	260
		Ruth	243	Victory	259
Oakley	143			Vigilance	293
Obedience	142	Sacrament	71	Viva	279
Offering	56	Sadness	287	Wales	262
Old Hundred	57	Safety	244	Warning	199
Old Trafford	170	Salem	225	Wasatch	267
Omega	254	Salford New	326	Watts	185
		Salutation	77	Watchman	230
Palmer	320	Salvation	72	Weber	268
Paradise	321	Samoa	257	Wellsville	83
Paris	62	Samson	76	Wilford	290
Parley	60	Sanford	197	Willard	84
Patience	148	Sanctity	73	Willes	328
Patten	324	Sarah	154	Windsor	85
Peace	180	Saturn	182	Winter Quarters	327
Pean	322	Selah	171	Wooburn	247
Penrose	272	Serenity	226	Woodruff	200
Peru	58	Solitude	75	Worship	160
Peter	59	Solomon	152	W. X.	86
Petition	241	Splendor	234	Wynona	280
Phelps	276	Springville	224		
Piety	147	Standard	227	Yates	291
Praise	94	St. Ann's	153	Zechariah	87
Pratt	144	Stella	79	Zephyr	288
Prayer	145	St. George	70	Zina	162
Preparation	61	St. Helens	183	Zion	231
Preston	323	St. John	74	Zion's Hill	161

METRICAL INDEX.

L. M.

	No.
Abram	7
Adoration	4
Advent	3
Albion	6
Alfred	12
Alman	8
Aloha	10
Antigua	11
Animation	1
Appleton	5
Arion	9
Assurance	2
Bereavement	17
Bethlehem	13
Beulah	16
Bradford	15
Brentford	14
Brigham	18
Bryant	19
China	21
Communion	20
Devotion	22
Eden	24
Edwinston	25
Emery	23
Eternity	26
Faith	27
Freedom	28
Gabriel	30
Gethsemane	29
Harmony	35
Harvest	31
Heavenly Home	37
Heber	32
Hosanna	36
Hudson	33
Hyrum	34
Immanuel	40
Irene	39
Israel	38
Jacob	41
Java	42
Jeanette	44
Jonathan	43
Joseph	45
Kimball	47
Kindness	46
Lehi	49
Light Divine	48
Lowell	50
Malachi	55
Meditation	51
Melody	54
Memory	52
Mother	53
Old Hundred	57
Offering	56
Paris	62
Parley	60
Peru	58
Peter	59
Preparation	61
Quietude	63
Redeemer	66
Redemption	67
Relief	68
Reliance	69
Restoration	64
Reverence	65
Sacrament	71
Salvation	72
Salutation	77
Samson	76
Sanctity	73
Solitude	75
Stella	79
Strength	78
St. George	70
St. John	74
Taylor	81
Truth	80
Vernon	82
Wellsville	83
Willard	84
Windsor	85
W. X.	86
Zechariah	87

C. M.

	No.
Alicia	99
Arizona	100
Atlantic	101
Bedford	103
Benediction	102
Calvary	111
Cannon	106
Cecil	104
Charity	109
Chorister	108
Confirmation	110
Contrition	112
Courage	105
Cowper	107
Creation	113
Dedication	116
Dorcas	115
Downham	114
Ebenezer	117
Enoch	118
Festival	122
Forgiveness	119
Fortitude	119
Friendship	121
Gratitude	124
Good Tidings	123
Hannah	126
Horace	128
Harold	125
Hartford	130
Home	129
Hope	127
Incarnation	131
Invocation	132
Lavinia	133
Maggie	137
Memorium	135
Mercy	138
Missionary	169
Mormon	136
Mt. Zion	134
Nephi	141
New Year	140
Norway	139
Oakley	143
Obedience	142
Patience	148
Piety	147
Pratt	144
Prayer	145
Promise	146
Quebec	149
Resurrection	150
Russell	151
Sarah	154
Solomon	152
St. Ann's	153
Thatcher	156
Tribute	157
Trinity	155
Union	158
Veneration	159
Worship	160
Zion's Hill	161
Zina	162

S. M.

	No.
Agnes	174
Alpha	175
Atonement	173
Bishop	176
Confidence	177
Gardner	178
Grace	179
Peace	180
Reunion	181
Saturn	182
St. Helens	183
Unity	184
Watts	185

L. M. D.

	No.
Carthage	89
Eucharist	88

L. P. M.

	No.
Justice	98

C. M. D.

	No.
Adoption	163
Blessing	164
Eliza R.	165
Farewell	166
Lyon	167
Majesty	168
Old Trafford	170
Selah	171
Utopia	172

S. M. D.

	No.
Martha	186

METRICAL INDEX.

6-8s.	No.
Comfort	90
Elliot	330
Inspiration	91
Jordan	93
Judah	92
Praise	94
Protection	95
Providence	96
Reflection	97

4-6s & 2-8s.	
Celebration	188
Compassion	190
Covenant	189
Cumorah	187
Deseret	192
Divinity	191
Felicity	193
Gladness	195
Greeting	194
Rapture	196
Sanford	197
Triumph	198
Warning	199
Woodruff	200

7s.	
Acacia	201
Azalia	202
Benson	203
Caleb	204
Deliverance	205
Eyra	206
Flora	207

8-7s.	
Ada	208
Ascription	209

6-7s.	
Burton	210
Finsley	211
Georgia	212
Testimony	213

8s & 7s.	
Adora	214
Bountiful	215
David	216
Gospel Light	217
Humanity	218
Jed	219
Laura	220
Minstrel	221
Rachael	222
Raymond	223
Salem	225
Serenity	226
Springville	224
Standard	227
Tamar	228
Transport	229
Watchman	230
Zion	231

8s & 7s D.	
Joyful Sound	232
Revelation	233
Splendor	234

8s, 7s & 4s.	No
Adieu	235
Gathering	238
Gloaming	236
Gospel	237
Herald	239
Invitation	240
Petition	241
Quincy	242
Ruth	243
Safety	244

8s.	
Edgeware	245
Tancie	246
Wooburn	247

8s & 7s. 6 Lines.	
Amphion	248

8s & 6s.	
Adina	249

7s & 6s D.	
Dimick	250
Elijah	251
Kolob	2, 2
Morgan	253
Omega	254
Supplication	255
Sweet Rest	256
Teasdale	258
Victory	259

7s & 6s.	
Samoa	257
Vesper	260

2-6s & 4 & 3-6s & 4.	
America	261
Wales	262

2-8s & 6s.	
Glory	263
Manti	264
New Hope	265
Rest	266
Wasatch	267
Weber	268

9s & 8s.	
Ballo	269
Eva	270
Fowler	271
Penrose	272
Temple	273

12s & 11s.	
Assembly	274
Elsinore	275
Lamentation	329
Phelps	276

11s & 10s.	
Brightness	277
Martyr	278

11s & 12s D.	
Viva	279

10s.	
Wynona	280

11s.	No.
Babylon	281
Fidelity	282
Goshen	283
Leone	285
Lyman	284
Sadness	287
Sweet Home	286
Zephyr	288

3-7s & 4.	
Marion	289

6, 6, 8, D.	
Wilford	290
Yates	291

3-8s & 7.	
Gray	292
Vigilance	293

8s & 9s.	
Roxie	294

4-7 & 4.	
Ure	295

2-8s & 7.	
Bellienall	296

6s & 7s.	
Repose	297

6s & 7s D.	
Patten	324

12s.	
Kirtland	298

P. M.	
Adam	300
Alpine	299
Caldwell	301
Cheltenham	302
Clayton	303
Davenport	305
Dawning	304
Erastus	307
Evan	306
Ezra	308
Far West	309
Glendale	310
Grantsville	311
Jaques	312
Joseph the Seer	314
Joshua	313
Liberty	315
Lucas	316
Michael	317
Naisbitt	318
New Salem	319
Palmer	320
Paradise	321
Pean	322
Preston	323
Rally	325
Salford New	326
Willes	328
Winter Quarters	327

INDEX TO FIRST LINES.

The hymns marked thus * are not specially arranged for, but may be sung to the tunes indicated. *a* Tune, "Cheer, boys, cheer;", *b* "To the west, to the west;" *c* "Star spangled banner."

First Line	No.
Again we meet around, etc.,	13
A poor way faring man, etc.,	34
A Saint! and is the title mine	149
Adieu, my dear brethren,etc.,	247
Adieu to the city, etc.,	329
Afflicted Saints, to Christ,etc.	78
All hail the glorious day	193
All hail! the new born year...	194
All praise to our, etc............	158
All you that love, etc............	40
An angel came down, etc.....	307
An angel from on high.........	187
A holy angel from on high...	18
And are we yet alive............	183
Another day has fled, etc......	51
Arise! arise! with joy survey..	55
Arise my soul, arise.............	190
Arise, O glorious Zion..........	259
As the dew, from heaven, etc.	215
At first the babe of Bethlehem	260
Author of faith,Eternal Word	27
*Awake! O ye people,etc.........	275
Awake! ye Saints of God, etc.	84
Away with your fears, etc. ...	306
Behold the Great Redeemer.	71
Be it my only wisdom here...	263
Before Jehovah's glorious,etc	43
Behold, the great, etc............	38
Behold the Lamb of God......	191
Behold the Mount, etc.........	14
Behold the mountain, etc....	161
Behold, the Savior comes......	181
Behold thy sons, etc.............	110
Beloved brethren,sing his,etc	155
Behold! the harvest, etc.........	31
Before all lands in east or west	296
Captain of Israel's host, etc...	95
Cease, ye fond parents, etc...	90
Cheer, Saints, cheer, etc.	*a*
Children of Zion, awake, etc.	284
Come, all ye Saints, etc.........	146
Come, all ye Saints who, etc.	114
Come, all ye sons of God,etc.	305
Come, all ye sons of Zion......	258
Come, come, ye Saints, etc...	327
Come, dearest Lord. etc....	22, 189
Come, go with me, etc...........	302
Come hither, all ye weary,etc	37
Come, Holy Ghost, etc.........	157
Come, let us anew, our, etc...	316
Come, let us purpose, etc.....	268
Come, let us sing, etc...........	124
Come, listen to a, etc............	106
Come, O thou King of kings.	197
Come, thou Desire, etc.........	99
Come, follow me, etc............	23
Come, thou glorious day,etc.	243
Come to me, etc....................	298
Come we that love, etc.	175, 185
Creation speaks, etc.............	42
Daniel's wisdom may I know.	211
Do we not know, etc............	74
Down by the river's, etc........	92
Dark is the human mind......	2
Deseret! Deseret! 'Tis, etc...	*b*
Do what is right, etc.............	304
Earth is the place where,etc.	12
Earth, with her, etc...............	213
Earthly happiness is fleeting.	222
Ere long the vail will, etc......	80
Except the Lord conduct, etc	267
Farewell all earthly, etc...253,	256
Farewell, my kind, etc..........	63
Farewell, our friends, etc......	257
Farewell, ye servants, etc.....	73
Father, how wide Thy, etc...	154
Father in heaven, etc............	162
For the strength, etc.............	311
From all that dwell, etc........	57
From Greenland's icy, etc...	251
*From the regions, etc............	307
Gently raise the sacred, etc...	295
Give us room that we, etc.....	206
Glorious things are sung,etc.	234
Glorious things of Thee, etc.	231
Glory to God on high...........	262
Glory to Thee my God, etc...	19
*Go ye Gospel heralds, go.....	210
Go, ye messengers of glory...	237
Go, ye messengers of heaven	229
God moves in a mysterious...	107
God of all consolation, etc...	102
God spake the word, etc......	24
Great God, attend while, etc.	47
Great God, indulge, etc.	4
Great God, to Thee, etc........	21
Great is the Lord! 'Tis, etc...	117
Great Spirit, listen, etc.........	280
Guide us, O thou Great, etc..	236
How great the wisdom, etc...	136
Hail! bright millennial, etc....	264
Hail to the brightness, etc....	277
Happy the man who finds,etc	58
Happy the souls who, etc.....	15
Hark! from afar a funeral,etc	266
Hark! listen to the gentle,etc	35
How dark and gloomy, etc...	67
Hark! listen to the trumpeters	105
Hark! the songs of Jubilee....	203
Hark! ten thousand, etc.......	299
Hark! ye mortals, etc...........	212
Haste glorious day, etc.........	59
He died! the great, etc..........	56
High on the mountain top....	192
Ho, ho, for the Temple's, etc..	273
Hosanna to the great Messiah	36
How have the nations, etc....	159
How are thy servants, etc. ...	119
How beauteous are their feet.	180
How firm a foundation, etc...	282
How fleet the precious, etc...	62
How foolish to the carnal,etc.	60
How great the joy, etc..........	10
*How often in sweet, etc........	287
How swift the months, etc...	318
How pleasant 'tis to see.......	291
How pleased and blessed,etc.	290
How sweet communion, etc..	20
How will the Saints, etc.......	134
I have no home, etc..............	75
If you could hie to Kolob.....	252
I know that my Redeemer,etc.	66
I long to breathe, etc............	129
I saw a mighty angel fly.......	100
I'll praise my Maker, etc......	94
I'll serve the Lord, etc.........	165
In ancient times a man of God	65
In Jordan's tide, etc..............	93
Inspirer of the ancient Seers.	91
In the sun and moon, etc......	204
Israel, Israel, God is calling...	238
Israel awake, etc.......... 322,	323
Jehovah, Lord of heaven,etc.	139
Joy to the world! the Lord's	137
Jesus, from whom all, etc.....	25
Jesus, mighty King in Zion...	223
Jesus, once of humble birth..	205
Jesus,thou all-redeeming,etc.	132
Judges,who rule the world,etc	98
Know this that every soul,etc.	28
Let earth and heaven agree...	188
Let every mortal ear attend..	122
Let Judah rejoice, etc..........	279
Let sinners take their course.	174
Let us pray, gladly pray.......	324
Let Zion in her beauty rise...	168
Let those who would be, etc.	120
Let earth's inhabitants rejoice	44
Lift up your heads, etc.........	130
Lord,let Thy Holy Spirit now	143
Lord when iniquities abound	121
Lord, dismiss us, etc............	241
Lord, make Thy mercy, etc..	176
Lord,Thou hast searched,etc.	30
Lord, Thou wilt hear, etc. 104,	169
Lord, we come before, etc....	201

INDEX TO FIRST LINES.

First line	No.
Lo! on the water's brink, etc.	142
Lo! the Gentile chain, etc.	227
Lo! the mighty God, etc.	242
*May the grace of Christ, etc.	224
May we, who know, etc.	115
*Men of God! go take, etc.	238
'Mid scenes of confusion, etc.	286
Mortals awake! with angels.	131
Mourn not the dead who, etc.	150
My Father in heaven, etc.	308
My God, the spring, etc.	147
My soul is full of peace, etc.	61
*Now he's gone, etc.	220
Now let us rejoice, etc.	276
Now we'll sing with one, etc.	202
Now, is the voice, etc.	249
O awake my slumbering, etc.	221
*O'er the gloomy hills, etc.	239
*O fear not brother, etc.	58
O God! our help, etc.	127
O God, th' Eternal Father.	255
O God, thou God, etc.	156
O God, thou great, etc.	113
Our God, we raise to thee.	261
O give me back my Prophet.	89
O! happy is the man, etc.	152
O happy home! etc.	265
O Lord of hosts, etc.	109
O happy souls who pray.	196
O Jesus! the giver.	283
*O Lord, do thou, etc.	c
O Lord, do thou thy gifts, etc.	163
O Lord, our Father, etc.	41
O Lord, our sovereign King.	195
O Lord! responsive, etc.	5
O, my Father, thou that, etc.	233
On the mountain tops, etc.	240
Once more, my soul, etc.	133
Once more we come, etc.	160
O Saints, have you seen, etc.	c
O say what is truth, etc.	312, 313
O stop and tell me, red man.	250
O Thou, at whose almighty.	82
O Thou at whose supreme, etc.	108
O Thou who hast promised.	285
Our Father, in the, etc.	164
O ye mountains high, etc.	315
*O, who that has searched, etc.	319
*O Zion, when I think on thee	34
O Lord, preserve thy, etc.	171
Peace, troubled soul, etc.	16
*Praise God from whom, etc.	57
Praise to God, immortal, etc.	207
Praise to the man, etc.	278
Praise ye the Lord, etc.	6
Praise ye the Lord, 'tis good.	8
Prayer is the soul's, etc.	145
Redeemer of Israel.	319
Repent, ye Gentiles all	189
Rest for the weary soul.	297

First line	No.
Satan's empire long, etc.	248
Salvation, sacred word, etc.	72
See! all creation joins.	182
See how the morning sun.	177
See the mighty angel, etc.	228
Shall I for fear, etc.	76
Should you feel inclined, etc.	214
Sing to the great, etc.	140
Sister, thou wast mild, etc.	220
Softly beams, etc.	226
Sons of Michael, etc.	317
Spirit of faith come down.	173
Stars of morning shout, etc.	289
Sweet is the peace, etc.	148
Sweet is the work, etc.	77
Sweetly may the blessed, etc.	224
School thy feelings, etc.	218
There's a feast of fat, etc.	301
The curse of God on man, etc.	118
*The child we dedicate, etc.	21
The day is past and gone.	179
Thou dost not weep, etc.	17
Though deep'ning trials, etc.	69
*This earth shall be, etc.	300
This earth was once, etc.	300
Thou earth, wast once, etc.	118
To Father, Son, etc.	153
Torn from our friends, etc.	86
The gallant ship is under, etc.	166
The glorious day is rolling on	141
The Gospel standard, etc.	170
This house we dedicate, etc.	116
The glorious Gospel light, etc.	123
The glorious plan which, etc.	81
The God that others, etc.	320
This God is the God, etc.	246
The great and glorious, etc.	9
Think gently of the erring one	138
The happy day has rolled on	1
There is a place in Utah.	328
Though in the outward, etc.	330
The Lord imparted, etc.	294
The Lord my pasture, etc.	96
The morning breaks, etc.	33
The morning flowers, etc.	53
This morning in silence, etc.	287
Think not when you, etc.	269
Though now the nations, etc.	49
Though nations rise, etc.	126
The night is wearing fast away	219
The pure testimony, etc.	309
The red man ceased, etc.	280
The rising sun has chased, etc.	48
The Seer, The Seer, etc.	314
*The shepherds have, etc.	281
The silver, gold, etc.	151
The solid rocks were rent, etc.	87
The Spirit of God, etc.	274
The sun that, etc.	288
The time is far spent, etc.	310
The time is nigh, etc.	70
The towers of Zion, etc.	85

First line	No.
The trials of the, etc.	292, 293
*The Upper California, etc.	320
To Him who reigns on high.	178
To Him who made the world	198
*To leave my dear friends.	288
To Thee, O God, etc.	167
Truth reflects upon, etc.	217
'Twas on that dark, etc.	29
'Twas the commission, etc.	32
Up, arouse thee, etc.	325
Up, awake, ye defenders, etc.	272
Unveil thy bosom, etc.	68
Wake, O wake the world, etc.	230
Waked from my bed, etc.	26
We're not ashamed to, etc.	125
Weep not for him, etc.	135
We have met, etc.	216
We'll sing the songs of Zion.	254
Weep, weep not for me, Zion.	321
Welcome, best of all, etc.	225
What fair one is this, etc.	275
What was witnessed, etc.	232
What wond'rous scenes, etc.	7
What wond'rous things, etc.	39
When all thy mercies, etc.	128
When earth in bondage, etc.	3
When first the glorious, etc.	303
When God's own people, etc.	46
When Joseph his brethren.	245
When Joseph saw his, etc.	45
When quiet in my house, etc.	97
When restless on my bed, etc	52
We here approach, etc.	88
We'll sing all hail, etc.	111
When shall we all meet, etc.	210
When sickness clouds, etc.	172
When time shall be no more.	199
When worn by sickness, etc.	128
Where the voice, etc.	209
Who are these arrayed, etc.	208
With all my powers, etc.	83
*With cheerful hearts, etc.	293
We thank thee, O God, etc.	271
What though the Gentiles, etc	326
With joy we own thy, etc.	112
While on these emblems, etc.	50
Ye Elders of Israel, etc.	281
Ye chosen Twelve, etc.	54
Ye children of our God.	184
Ye Gentile nations, etc.	11
Ye ransomed of our God.	200
Ye Saints who dwell, etc.	101
Ye simple souls who stray.	186
Ye sons of men, a feeble race	103
*Ye who are called to labor, etc	253
Ye wond'ring nations, etc.	144
Yes my native land, etc.	235
Your sweet little rosebud, etc	270
Ye differing, jarring, etc.	64
Zion stands with hills, etc.	244

www.ingramcontent.com/pod-product-compliance
Lightning Source LLC
Chambersburg PA
CBHW031338230426
43670CB00006B/372